D1285311

the last jews
of
eastern europe

text by Yale Strom
illustrations by
Brian Blue and Yale Strom
with a preface by George Schwab

Philosophical Library
New York

The author acknowledges the following works, which were used as references for information contained in the text:

...And You Shall Tell Your Son...Jewish Customs and Ceremonies in Hungary, text by Sandor Scheiber, Photographs by Tamas Fener. Translated by Joseph W. Wiesenberg. Budapest: Revai Printing House, 1984.
Encyclopedia of Judaica. Jerusalem: Keter Publishing House, 1972.
Pictorial History of the Jewish People, by Nathan Ausubel. New York: Crown Publishers, Inc., 1954.
Polish Jewry: History and Culture, by Marian Fuks, Zygmunt Hoffman, Maurycy Horn, and Jerzy Tomaszewski. Translated by Bogna Piotrowska and Lech Petrowica. Warsaw: Interpress Publisher, 1982.
The Shtetl Book, by Diane K. Roskies and David G. Roskies. New York, Jerusalem: KTAV Publishing House, Inc., 1979, 2nd revised edition.
The Vanished Worlds of Jewry, by Raphael Patai, picture research by Eugene Rosow with Vivian Kleiman. New York: Macmillan Publishing Co., Inc., 1980.
The War against the Jews, 1933-45, by Lucy Dawidowicz. London: Weidenfeld & Nicolson, 1975; New York: Penguin Books, 1975.

Library of Congress Cataloging in Publication Data

Strom, Yale.
  The last Jews of Eastern Europe.

  1. Jews—Europe, Eastern—Pictorial works.   2. Holocaust survivors—Europe, Eastern—Pictorial works.   3. Europe, Eastern—Description and travel—Views.
I. Blue, Brian.   II. Title.
DS 135.E83S75   1986   947'.0004924   86-25354
ISBN 0-8022-2520-9

preface

The story the pictures convey is not just any story but that of a people burdened by trials and tribulations of thousands of years of history. The worn faces and worn books, the neglected and destroyed synagogues and cemeteries, the painful smiles and sad laughter, the saga the photographs encapsulate is always the same: the sorrowful and yet dramatically unprecedented narrative of a people who, despite dispersion, persecution, and systematic slaughter, continue to live and to contribute to the progress of civilization and culture.

The photographs stir deep emotions and raise many questions, foremost, perhaps, the extent to which the tragedy of the Jewish people can be interpreted to be the central Christian problem with which Christianity has still not come to terms. Specifically, can the Holocaust, Christianity run amok, be explained as an example of parricide, a convulsive and most extreme endeavor to erase Christianity's historical and religious roots? Or can it be construed as a reaction to a feeling that the carriers of the intellectual spirit in Germany since the nineteenth century were Jews with whom, Germans felt, they could not compete, thus leading them to take refuge in the soul? Unable to oppose the onslaught of the intellect in this domain as well, the soul finally opted to defend itself by erecting gas chambers.

Interpretations aside, given Jewry's impact on the course of history—that is, by having furnished us with monotheism—Jewry provided the spiritual and moral foundations on which our civilization and culture rest. Since it has supplied us with an incredibly rich stream of intellectual productions, the loss of genius of this people, minuscule in number, is surpassed only by the unfathomableness of the dimension of the human tragedy that a number like 6,000,000 can symbolize. How many future Spinozas and Bubers,

Mendelssohns and Mahlers, Modiglianis and Chagalls, Kafkas, Freuds, and Einsteins have found their resting place in gas chambers, concentration camps, ghettos, and elsewhere?

What has become of that part of Europe that is relatively *Juden-rein*, clean of Jews? The answer the photographs provide is unequivocal. Whether it is a *shtetl*, a village or town, or centers like Vilna, Krakow, Prague, or Riga, Warsaw, Budapest, or Odessa, the story is always the same: the zest and vigor that characterized these once brilliant centers of cultural, intellectual, scientific, and commercial life to Jew and Christian alike is gone. There is a question that is, however, nagging. Can the vigor, vitality, and zest that still characterizes Jewish life in East Central Europe suffice to spark a renaissance, a rejuvenation? Logic says no. Yet history is known to deceive reason.

George Schwab
Professor of History
City University of New York
Graduate Center

contents

a tree still stands

East European Jewry. I shudder to write the phrase. I am astonished to note that it exists today, that it has survived, endured a millennium unbelievable in its lack of mercy: There was the casual anti-Semitisim of neighbors envious of the Jews' ability to thrive during the numberless times of restrictions by potentates, despots and democratic governments. Then there was the incomparable Holocaust, which cannot be justly spoken of but by recitation of facts and presentations of photographs. Then there was the aliya to Israel, fulfillment of a Jewish dream and the bleeding of the great Jewish artery that is East European Jewry.

I am in awe because it still exists today, and I leap in the air at the chill, the bumps on my skin that I feel right now, because it *does*, it *does*. Ephraim of Budapest, circumcised at the age of forty-one, danced and served wine and honeycakes to his friends when the doctor he had brought from London finished the ritual. I feel as he did. I feel honored to be a Jew and to know that Ephraim, his family, and thousands like him keep kehillot robust throughout the Soviet Union, Poland, Czechoslovakia, Hungary, Romania, Yugoslavia, and Bulgaria.

They are alive and living in the tradition—young ones and old ones. This book of stories and photographs demonstrates that. Brian and I had the great fortune to meet the people of these stories, to reach out to them, to watch them perform the ancient rituals, watch children two years old take the first steps of the tradition in a Jewish school serving a kosher lunch, watch a woman of ninety-three glow as she ate her kosher lunch and spoke, in both Yiddish and English, of what she had seen.

These people are alive in Eastern Europe, living as Jews, without assimilation.

Our book records the three great blows to East European Jewry:

the historical persecution of the Jews who suffered the envy of their neighbors; the slaughter of millions of Jews during World War II in the countries the Nazis desecrated; and the loss of the Jews who accepted the aliya to Israel, their new lives in the Promised Land further decimating the kehillot of Eastern Europe.

This book records, too, how the Jews of Eastern Europe laugh, weep, and sing. And oh, how they do those things! Please come and watch them.

I offer my thanks to a group of young Jews I met in 1978 in the Moscow Central Synagogue. It was Purim, and they wanted to talk to me because I was an American Jew. They knew that I belonged to another arm of the tradition. But they recognized KGB agents standing nearby, and took me to a small park. There they held my hands and had me join them in Hebrew and Yiddish folk songs. A guitar played and the cold of the afternoon was burned away. Cold, I would discover, is so much of the life of the kehillot of the Eastern Bloc. And talk and song are so much of the warmth that keeps the feet and hands from frostbite.

I hope those young Jews, now older, read and watch this book. They compelled me to make it.

There was a preparatory journey in 1981, centered on Jewish music, especially klezmer music. Then, on October 30, 1984, the journey that led to this book began, and continued for five months. Brian Blue, a photographer with an acute eye, journeyed with me. I am grateful that he did, as you will be who open this book. He is *not* a Jew, and I believe that that gave his eye a singular sharpness.

I confess I was eager to tell you more of our personal journey. But the power of the story of the kehillot forbad me. Therefore, I have tried to disappear. I hope I have succeeded. I have tried to make the stories live, as the photographs freeze moments in time and carry with them their past, present, and future.

The living history is what matters. You will see it in Ephraim, the Cojacaru sisters, Shamash David of Plovdiv, Zipporah, Zoran the soldier. You will see it in the synagogues, the Jewish clubs, the kosher kitchens, and the cemeteries. I hope I have not intruded too much.

I would like to thank all the Jews Brian and I met while traveling through Eastern Europe. These people, through their most generous hospitality—their "menshlekheit"—opened the doors of their synagogues, kosher kitchens, clubs, and homes offering food, warmth, and a glimpse into their past and present.

Throughout our travels we were befriended by many, and without them our task would have been much more difficult: people like Genia Lis, Krystna Piekarska, and Ludmilla Pollack, who allowed us to stay with them; and Bea Sommersguter, who gave us the full use of her darkroom in Vienna, where we developed our first sixty-nine rolls of film.

My enthusiasm for Yiddish culture was nurtured at home and developed while I studied at the YIVO Institute and New York

University. Teachers and friends such as Dr. Barbara Kirshenblatt-Gimblett, Dr. Jack Kugelmass, and Prof. Laurin Raiken provided advice and guidance.

I also thank my parents, David and Phyllis Strom, who gave me a solid and traditional Jewish upbringing and the support and opportunity which enabled me to learn to play the violin. Klezmer music was the bond between myself and the people in this book.

Finally, I want to express my wonder at and thanks for George Schwab's brilliant Preface. It provides the correct context for this story of pictures. But what it does most astoundingly is frame the only right question: can the vitality of life in Eastern Europe spark a renaissance, can Jewry there, to use the words of Faulkner in his Nobel speech, "not only survive but prevail"? We did not find much logic in Eastern Europe, just the chill of experiencing abundant life.

Thank you for opening this book. You won't be sorry you met these people, that you saw these sights inside.

U.S.S.R.

kishinev

A smallish man quickly paces a narrow street toward a large, nondescript, blue-gray building. He darts inside a gate and disappears out of the Kishinev afternoon.

Above the gate a window reveals a Magen David hanging within a room of the building. A few moments later, the man—who had not wanted to be conspicuous as one going to study and prayer—is studying the Talmud. He is inside a synagogue. He is surrounded by the living history and tradition of Jewish life: the eternal light over the ark, the candlesticks on the bima, tallisim draped over the backs of wooden benches, and well-tattered siddurim strewn over the seats of the benches.

An older man enters, and joins in peaceful study. Safe in this room of Jewish history, the man who had been furtive in the street reveals himself to be a young yeshiva student.

After services another day, Shmuel, shamash of the synagogue, explains the care congregants take in this city. Refusing to be photographed, he says: "Itzkhak, you are my friend, but I don't know if the guards at the border will take your film." He speaks of the authorities and his fear is that the congregants will be questioned and harassed by those authorities if photographs are discovered—photographs of religious activities frowned on by the state.

Among the older Jews, closer to the burning anti-Semitism of the earlier twentieth century than the younger ones, and more in touch with the historical anti-Semitism than the younger ones as well, there is little resentment of concealment that they feel is required to practice their religion. They believe that the Western press makes too much of Soviet government interference. They cite, with resignation more than heat, examples of racial and anti-Semitic problems in the United States.

Older Jews attend synagogue services more consistently than younger Jews. A twice-daily minyan consists of twelve to fifteen men—most of them older. Following each morning service, a kiddush and a pick-me-up schnapps are served. The history breathes here as surely as it does in the siddurim.

While synagogue worship is the most visible form of Jewish expression in Kishinev and the rest of the Soviet Union, wary Jews live their religious life more robustly. Within careful mantles of suspicion, groups celebrate Shabbat and holidays and festivals, study Hebrew and Yiddish, hear concerts and lectures, and give each other moral and material support in their lives as Jews.

The synagogue where the lone young student studies the Talmud and the old ones attend minyan is Beit Knesset Kishinev, built in 1884. It is the only one that has not been closed by the government since the end of World War II. Before the war, there had been more than fifty synagogues in the city.

As early as the years following the destruction of the Second Temple in 70 C.E. Jews passed through the city. But, Jewish history in Kishinev did not formally begin until 1774, with the formation of the formal kehilla and a burial society. In 1816, the first synagogue, the Great Synagogue, was built. Two years later, Kishinev became capital of Bessarabia, under Russian rule, and the kehilla grew rapidly.

Jews became important in the garment and timber trades, as well as in commerce and handicrafts. By 1847, their population was 10,509, growing by 1897 to 50,237, forty-six percent of the total population. Many Jews became prosperous, but a large segment of the kehilla was poor, since those Jews were skilled in occupations forbidden Jews by the Russian government. In 1898, welfare organizations joined to form the Society for Aid of the Poor.

On April 6 and 7, 1903, the Jews of Kishinev were victims of a large Easter pogrom. It was preceded by a poisonous barrage of anti-Semitic articles in the local paper. Hatred of Jews reached a fever pitch when the body of a Christian child was found. Jews were accused of ritual murder.

As a result of an international outcry against those who had instigated the pogrom, the Tsar ordered them to be tried. Lenient sentences were imposed, and a second pogrom followed in 1905. The kehilla of Kishinev then lost its first substantial number of Jews. Of this mass exodus, most landed in the United States.

Kishinev (Chisinau) had once been part of the Romanian province of Bessarabia, and it returned to Romanian rule in 1918, to remain until 1940. Jews were treated no better, and the kehilla struggled to survive. Zionist organizations became active, and Hebrew and Yiddish flourished in homes, newspapers, and books.

Then, in June 1940, the Soviet Union annexed Bessarabia. Many Zionists and wealthy Jews were transported to Siberia, and Jewish institutions were closed. A month later German and Romanian troops occupied the city.

Between July and October 1941, 10,000 Jews were slaughtered by the German Einsatzgruppen units and Romanian gendarmerie. On October 4, 1941, the deportations to Transnistria began, Jews being sent to labor and extermination camps. Of a prewar population of 65,000, only 12,000 returned to Kishinev after the war.

Since the end of Nazi terror and the resurgence of Soviet control, the kehilla population has continued to decline. For the most part the young Jews with families who maintain their Jewishness are not looking to remain in Kishinev.

Gregori and Elizabeth Leiderman stand under the quiet light of a street lamp near the remaining synagogue. They explain why they only visit the old building on the High Holidays. It is, they reveal, infiltraded by government informants. This despite the fact (or because of the fact) that the synagogue is where most practicing Jews in Kishinev, as in the other cities of the Soviet Union, meet Jews from the West.

The older Jews study and reflect on their history. But the younger ones want to know of Jews throughout the world, and of how Jewish life is going in the late twentieth century. They therefore risk being suspected by the government—which does not distinguish between dissidence and curiosity.

Caught in this bind, the Leidermans have waited nine years for permission to emigrate to Israel. During this wait, they help other families keep their Jewishness alive. They know that Jewish culture is expressed in thousands of Jewish homes in the Soviet Union. They also know that as soon as they can they will take their ten-year-old daughter, Ina, from the kehilla of Kishinev to Israel, and that thousands of other young families will also take their children to Israel—away from the physical history of Eastern Europe.

In the Leidermans' apartment we meet Elizabeth's gypsy friend, Nicolai Radu. Having been a musician for forty years and having played with Jewish klezmorim throughout Moldavia and Bessarabia during those years, he speaks Yiddish. He is a friend of Elizabeth, and often visits their home. As the Leidermans speak and Nicolai plays, there are 7,000 Jews in the city. And the Leiderman family is one of 200 families waiting for permission to leave.

Jasha, assistant to the shamash, is not waiting to leave. He always can be found cleaning the synagogue grounds. Jasha always seems jovial. He has a good friend, Moshe, whose job is to prepare the dead for burial.

But the old Jewish cemetery, nearly 120 years old, is no longer in use. It was closed in 1980, forcing Jews to use a small section of the Christian burial grounds.

The Jewish cemetery is uncared for and

the subject of vandalism. At night it becomes a drinking place. Men climb the fence and sit on the stones. The gravestones are defaced, and the cemetery is littered with empty vodka bottles and the debris of these nightly gatherings.

Odessa

It is morning in the synagogue, and a woman asks the shamash to recite Kaddish for her dead husband. She also asks that his name be placed under one of the synagogue's memorial lights. When all is done, the shamash receives a small fee. In Odessa, ritual services, including the very personal ones, go on—as have Jewish services since before Europe was civilized.

Every day services are held, and on Saturday as many as sixty men and twenty women attend. One man, Meyer, comes to minyan wearing a medal of valor he received for defending the Soviet Union against the Nazis. He is one of many congregants who survived the war and feel sincere gratitude to the Soviet government for its protection during the German invasion.

Unlike Kishinev, in the clear, lighted air, as many as 3,000 Jews overflow the synagogue into the courtyard and nearby streets, listening to prayers on loudspeakers.

But this is during the High Holidays. As is true in Kishinev, in Odessa most forms of Jewish expression take place in the privacy of the home. There are few public reminders of the days when Odessa was an important center of Yiddish culture. On a downtown street is a poster, in Russian, on a sidewalk billboard announcing a coming production of a play by Sholem Aleichem. In the old Jewish quarter, one of the streets bears the author's name. But this street runs into another street that is named for Bogdan Chmielnicki, the seventeenth-century Cossack leader infamous for his virulent anti-Semitism.

The Jews of Odessa have survived hundreds of years of tolerance and intolerance. They traveled and traded around the Black Sea coast in ancient times, having encounters with more than one Cossack. Documents indicate a permanent kehilla in Odessa in 1794. A grain industry burgeoned in the 1830s, and Jews began to work the docks as loaders, weighers, and sorters. By 1910, more than 80 percent of the grain companies were owned by Jews.

Culture grew with commerce. In the late nineteenth century Odessa was the most western of all the communities in the Pale of Settlement. A center of Haskala and later of secular Jewish education, the city's learning centers became models of a general and modern Hebrew education. The teachers H. N. Bialik, Hayyim Tchernowitz, and Joseph Klausner drew Jewish students from throughout Russia.

And Odessa became a world center for Hebrew literature, attracting aggressive young men who rallied around various literary and artistic movements, and who strengthened and intensified various political parties. Until the Russian Revolution, Odessa sat at the pinnacle of Jewish intellectual life in southeastern Europe.

With the Revolution, though, assimilation began to grow. By 1926, 77 percent of Jewish pupils attended Russian schools, only 22 percent Yiddish schools. Leading artists, musicians, professors, and intellectuals fled Odessa for Western Europe or Palestine. But there were still sixty synagogues in the city.

Then came June 21, 1941 and the invasion of the Germans and the Romanians. Refugees from Bukovina, Bessarabia, and the Western Ukraine swelled the Jewish population of Odessa. Jews joined the Red Army and fled to the cities of Taskent and Baku, farther east. A two-month siege ensued, leading to the occupation of the city on October 16, 1941.

The massacres began while 80,000 to 90,000 Jews were still in the city. There were mass shootings, bombings, and burnings. Those who survived were deported to Transnistria. And on February 23, 1942,

Odessa was proclaimed *Judenrein* by the Nazis.

The Red Army liberated Odessa on April 10, 1944. Three thousand Jews had survived. In the days after the war, survivors from throughout the Soviet Union made Odessa their home. By 1985 the city's Jewish population had climbed to 120,000.

When the war ended eleven synagogues remained. Now there is one. It is eighty years old, and its history is entwined with a matzoh-baking factory next door to it. A fire nearly destroyed that factory; the fire spread to the synagogue, which had to be rebuilt in 1971.

Today, as it shares the synagogue courtyard, that matzoh factory bakes sixty tons of matzohs from Tu B'Shevat until Passover.

This is about one pound for every Jew in Odessa. The synagogue obtains money from selling this matzoh, which helps pay for the upkeep of the shul and cemetery, with a small salary remaining for the synagogue officials.

And as the minyan survives daily in the synagogue, so does the memory of Odessa's literary past. The city was the final home of Mendele Mokher Sefarim, father of modern Yiddish literature. The Nazis destroyed his library. But his gravesite is in the traditional Jewish cemetery, twenty minutes from the center of town.

The Nazis failed to destroy it.

poland

WARSAW

It is Wednesday night and, as on every Wednesday night, Monika Krajewska and her husband Stacik are holding a gathering for all those who care to come.

Those who come include young Jewish students, artists, musicians, and professionals. They know that Monika, a Catholic converted to Judaism, has earned an international reputation for her recent book on the remnants of Jewish cemeteries throughout Poland. Jewish topics including Israel are discussed. In the most deeply Catholic country of Eastern Europe Judaism survives.

Byzantium, the Moslem East, and the ancient Jewish kingdom of Khazaria sent the first Jews to the area that would become Poland late in the tenth century. Hard upon this came the Crusades and indiscriminate massacres following the Black Plague, which sent thousands of Jews fleeing from Germany and Bohemia to seek refuge in Poland. They brought skills as merchants, traders, artisans, moneylenders, and craftsmen. They also brought their Judeo-German dialect, the precursor of Yiddish.

In 1264 Prince Boleslav granted the Jews a charter of privileges. It guaranteed their economic rights and protected their lives, property, and synagogues. And it gave them an extraordinary degree of autonomy. Casimir the Great (1333-1370) extended these privileges.

Despite anti-Semitic attitudes among the nobles, burgers, and clergy, Polish Jewry thrived. By the sixteenth century, they had made Poland the undisputed leader in Ashkenazi religious scholarship, with rabbinical giants such as Moses Isserles (1530-1572) in the forefront. The Polish yeshivot became so numerous that the majority of Jewish males knew both Hebrew and Aramaic and were well-versed in the Talmud and the commentaries.

Allowed considerable autonomy, Polish Jews established a countrywide organization of the kehillot called the Council of Four Lands. Representatives of Greater and Lesser Poland, Polia, Galicia, and Volhynia met twice each year. They governed all aspects of Jewish life for nearly one and three-quarters centuries (1592-1764). Thereafter the Polish Diet ordered Jewish congresses to be discontinued.

In 1648-1649, Cossack Bodgan Chmielnicki led a slaughter of 200,000 Jews. Pogroms led by the Haidamak peasantry occurred one hundred years later. The eighteenth century also saw the beginning of the Hasidic movement, founded in the Carpathian mountains by Israel ben Eliezer (1700-1760), better known as the Baal Shem Tov. With its joyful, impassioned approach to prayer and God, the mystical piety of Hasidism spread throughout Poland and all Eastern Europe, ultimately influencing the character of shtetl life more than any other philosophy.

The first partition of Poland occurred in 1772, and the Polish Republic was not established until 1918. Meanwhile, in 1881, pogroms broke out in Volhynia, Podolia, Chernigov, and Poltava. Thousands of Jews were killed and other thousands escaped to the United States, England, Canada, and Latin America. The same period also saw the development of Zionism, the Jewish labor movement, and socialism, as well a revival of Hebrew.

More pogroms contributed to the general horror of World War I. The Versailles Peace Treaty tried to protect Jewish rights in the Polish state reborn after the war. But the new government limited Jewish participation in commercial life, and in many ways continued to encourage Polish anti-Semitism. Many Jews chose to leave Poland, draining the kehillot of vitality. Jewish schools began to reflect increasing fragmentation of the community. There were Yiddish secular schools of the Bund and the Po'alei Zion, Agudut Israel, and Mizrachi Polish-Hebrew elementary and secondary schools, and a huge Hebrew-language school system (45,000 students during the 1930s). Still, most Jewish children attended Polish state schools.

On September 1, 1939, 1.7 million German soldiers marched into Poland. Poland again was invaded on September 17, 1939, by the Soviet Red Army. By the end of the month, obviously overwhelmed, the country had capitulated, suffering division by the two invaders.

Jews sought refuge in Soviet-occupied Poland. Relief was short, as Germany invaded the Soviet Union on June 22, 1941.

The Holocaust revealed its most horrible face to Polish Jewry. The ghettos, concentration camps, and the gas chambers of Auschwitz, Treblinka, Sobibor, and elsewhere saw the murder of 3,000,000 Polish Jews. Incredible numbers of other Jews were sent to Poland from the rest of Nazi-occupied Europe so they could be exterminated with their Polish brethren.

In April 1940 the Germans began to build the walls of the Warsaw Ghetto. On October 2, all Jews or those with Jewish origins were ordered to move within the ghetto within six weeks. "Aryans" were to leave. Though the original ghetto covered 840 acres, including the Jewish cemetery, the area was reduced again and again.

Between 400,000 and 500,000 lived in the ghetto. Despite hunger, poverty, disease, and Nazi atrocities, ghetto Jews maintained schools and welfare institutions, and continued to sing and to read their sacred works.

Then came the mass deportations to Treblinka, beginning July 22, 1942. As many as 13,000 people were deported daily.

On April 13, 1943 the Warsaw Ghetto Uprising began, with the Jewish underground mounting a fierce resistance. But by May 16, 1943 the ghetto had been destroyed by German military units.

About fifty Jews who escaped to nearby forests formed a partisan unit. On January 17, 1945, Warsaw was liberated. Two hundred Jewish survivors crawled out of the rubble.

At the end of the war, there were about 250,000 Jews throughout Poland, the great majority of them refugees from other areas. This was to shrink to 35,000 by 1960, through emigration to Israel. In 1968, the Polish Communist government launched a major anti-Semitic campaign, leading to the last of the large-scale emigrations of Jews.

Today, Warsaw Jews are still going to the synagogue, eating at the kosher kitchen, attending the Warsaw Jewish State Theater. They also go to the various Jewish clubs—for lectures, music, films, plays, Yiddish cabaret, and to laugh, eat, drink, or play chess and cards, and simply to be together.

The clubs handle the day-to-day work of the kehilla's breathing: administration, burying the dead, cooking the food traditionally, distributing matzoh and wine during Passover.

It is evening at a student evangelical club. Wladyslaw Wojick hears klezmer music and feels the tradition. The Yiddish folk song "Dire Gelt" is played and sung, and Wladyslaw remembers hearing it as a young boy in Warsaw.

Later that night the actors and actresses of the experimental theater known as "Gardinicza," who incorporate Hasidic melodies in their theater music, ask to hear new Hasidic and Yiddish melodies. The music comes from the violin and the guitar together.

Some synagogues survive, complementing the vigor in the clubs. The Nozick Shul, the only synagogue left standing after the Warsaw Ghetto was razed, was refurbished in 1982. The Nazis used it as a stable, but once again it is a sacred building. Still, there is a minyan only on Shabbat.

It is Shabbat in the Nozick Shul. A man dressed in black with a long beard enters. He begins to kneel before the ark. He crosses himself while holding a large wooden cross, mumbling inaudible words. Congregants suspect mockery or perhaps madness. But no one disturbs the man, whatever his purpose. He soon leaves.

This Shabbat there are thirty-five men and three women, with the women in the rear of the congregation rather than upstairs. The visit of the man in black has dampened spirits and no one sings.

The end of the service comes and some women, peasants from the country, step through the door. Thinking they are in a church, they kneel and cross themselves. Then they realize where they are, smile apologies, and rush out.

It is a few days later at the kosher kitchen. Josef, who only recently began having his lunch there, has arrived. Josef is a collector of old Hebrew and Yiddish memorabilia, particularly books. He walks with a number of young people from the kitchen to his home where he has set aside space for his personal "library." He eagerly shows his collection of old books, photographs, coins, sheet music—artifacts from the history and culture of Polish Jewry.

He says he intends his collection to be a dowry, an enticement for a Jewish man to marry his seventeen-year-old daughter. Josef also reveals that he has written books on the theater, the working class, and the Bund.

The Jewish cemetery, dating from the eighteenth century, is clogged with brush and trees. Outside the ghetto's western wall, the thick growth once provided natural camouflage for smuggling between Jews and gentiles during the war. Armed resistance during the ghetto uprising also lasted longest here.

Today is the day of the funeral of Clara Erlich, seventy-seven, in her last years supervisor of Jewish dietary laws in the kehilla's kosher kitchen. Boleck, the caretaker, and his two assistants carry the coffin, intending to bury it before the people gather.

They lower the casket, but the hole is too narrow. Their solution is to beat the coffin with the heads of their shovels.

The casket begins to crack and two onlookers tell the workers to stop. The strangers pick and dig at the frozen ground, frantic to widen the grave. At last, the coffin can be forced into the ground, though at an angle. The final shovelful of dirt falls on the grave, and the funeral party arrives.

krakow

Zvi Segula is laughing. He also is playing the violin and singing in Yiddish while his daughter accompanies on the mandolin. He is the Yiddish teacher of Krakow.

Once each week, at the Jewish club, he teaches seven students, using an old text published by the Hebrew Publishing Company in 1920. An inventive, enthusiastic teacher, he adds simple conversational Yiddish and Yiddish folk songs to the lesson. And he often plays the fiddle as he sings the verses.

Once each week also, again in the Jewish club, Hebrew is taught. The teacher is a young, energetic Catholic, a university instructor who had taught himself Hebrew from old grammar books printed in Germany. He also had trained his ear by listening to Radio Jerusalem, transmitted from Israel for Jews in Europe, whenever he could. In his class are Jewish and Catholic students, and a few older, retired Jews. This week the weather is frigid in the normal classroom (the heater is broken), and the students cram into a tiny room of the club. When the lesson is over, the teacher and some students quaff a beer at the famous pub named Pivnicza (Cellar).

German Jews came to Krakow in the last half of the thirteenth century, attracted to the city by its location on the Vistula River.

Despite the anti-Semitism, they soon established themselves in Krakow. By 1407, in the heart of nearby Kazimierz, in its ghetto, they had built the Alte Shul, Poland's oldest existing synagogue. The famous Rema synagogue, originally built of wood by the father of Rabbi Moses Isserles, later rebuilt in stone, soon joined the magnificent Gothic-style Alte Shul.

After years of anti-Jewish restrictions and mob outbursts, in 1495 Jews were forced to leave Krakow, which was then the capital of Poland (and remained so until 1609). But they had already begun to establish one of the most important of the European kehillot there. Though forced to live in Kazimierz they continued to visit "their town." Into the sixteenth and first half of the seventeenth century, the Jews exiled to Kazimierz reflected cultural fame of Krakow.

Jewish "visits" to Krakow proper included Rabbi Isserles's establishment of Krakow as the center of rabbinic study. His most famous work adapts the Shulkhan Arukh to the needs of Ashkenazic Jews. This Talmudic learning spread throughout Poland.

With full legal emancipation and the unrestricted right to settle in Krakow (1867-1868) came the beginning of assimilation. A secular Jewish Religious Council began to oversee the entire infrastructure of the kehilla.

Within this situation, the kehilla helped Krakow create a cosmopolitan environment, with a wide array of economic opportunity, while still maintaining a vibrant Jewish cultural and religious life. The city was said to suit everyone from the Hasidim to the Maskilim, and Krakow attracted Jews from all over Eastern Europe in the late nineteenth and early twentieth centuries.

By 1931, twenty-six percent of Krakow's population was Jewish, 56,800 persons.

The Nazis occupied Krakow after the invasion of Poland in 1939. About 35,000 Jews managed to escape, first to Galicia, then to the Soviet Union. On March 21, 1949, the Nazis established a ghetto. Then came several "selections" of victims sent to the Belzec death camp. Meanwhile, thousands of other Jews died of starvation and disease. Then the ghetto was liquidated, in the middle of March 1943. Armed resistance, begun as early as the end of 1940, could not stop this tragedy.

After the war, about 3,000 Jews chose to live in the city, but not in any one area. Emigration has left only 600 Jews in Krakow as of 1985.

What was the old Jewish quarter is the kehilla headquarters, where Jewish life still centers. Two synagogues still are in use, Rema and the Temple. The kosher kitchen, the Jewish cultural house, and the Museum of Jewish History are housed in the former Alte Shul—which physically brings kehilla history back to the early, early days of glory.

The Jewish quarter itself still stands, a medieval relic. On Josefa and Isaak Streets, the ancient buildings recall a happier past.

Today it is, appropriately, cool and wet, a constant drizzle falling. Jerzy, coordinator of the Jewish club, and his friend, Joasha, are enjoying borscht, made by Joasha's father, Michel and taken with pumpkin seeds and sucking candy.

When the little meal is finished, Michel, an actor and singer, says goodbye to his daughter and her friend. The two men will sit in the Jewish quarter and reflect, in that gray place, under the drizzle.

WROClaw

Esther is a twinkling, generous-spirited woman who lives in a fourth-floor walk-up in an old building. She is serving a free lunch to Raphael ben Itzkhak Zileinski in the kosher kitchen in the old seminary courtyard. Across the hall of this building is the tiny synagogue where, each Friday night and Shabbat morning, minyan is held.

The kitchen charges the elderly poor Jews nothing for their meals; a small fee is charged others. Twice a month, the kitchen is served by a shokhet from Dzierzoniow.

This kitchen and the synagogue and the

visitors and the few elderly Jews who live in the small complex are all that remain of the first modern Jewish theological seminary. It was established by Rabbi Zachariah Frankel in 1854. Its construction was a high point in the long, arduous history of the city.

The first Jewish settlers of Wroclaw (or Breslau) were refugees fleeing Bohemia during the scourge of the Crusades from 1180 to 1208. In 1266 Jews in Breslau were ordered by Church authorities into what was probably the first compulsorily walled ghetto anywhere, "lest perchance the Christian people be, on this account, the more easily infected with superstition and depraved morals of the Jews dwelling among them."

Nevertheless, with the help of the Jewish community, Wroclaw became the largest city of the German province of Silesia, remaining so until the end of World War II.

By the eighteenth century, the Jewish community contained three economic groups: the Landjuden, who earned their livings as lessees of mills, breweries, and inns; the small businessmen, peddlers, traders, and merchants; and, the most priviledged and wealthiest of all, the suppliers of war armaments and developers of industry. These few families of wealth helped usher in the Haskalah movement that made the city the leading Jewish intellectual center in all Germany until 1938.

By 1933, when Hitler gained control of Germany, the Jewish population had reached 20,202. On November 11, 1938, the day after Kristalnacht, Jewish educational, cultural, and social activities were rudely disrupted. Jewish life began to suffocate. The last ordination at the Jewish Theological Seminary took place, clandestinely, on February 21, 1939.

Most Jews of this area, which they had made prosperous, perished in the concentration or extermination camps of Auschwitz, Sobibor, Theresienstadt.

After the war, the Soviet-controlled Polish government brought 52,000 repatriated Jews from Galicia and Sub-Carpathian Ruthenia, areas that had come under Soviet domination at war's end.

Hebrew schools were re-established, and a state-supported Yiddish elementary education helped resume Jewish life. But a tragic pogrom broke out in Kielce in 1946. Jews began to flee by the thousands. In subsequent years thousands more emigrated, mostly to Israel.

Nevertheless, today Wroclaw maintains the third-largest kehilla in Poland, 300 to 400 strong. Half of these are nominally involved in the monthly cultural activities of the focal point of kehilla life—the Jewish club.

Most days, eight men come to the club office to read newspapers, listen to the radio, and just relax. Nights bring more men—both Jewish and gentile—to play cards, watch television, schmooze, and eat snacks.

The kosher kitchen is situated on the grounds of the seminary that once had a faculty which included leaders of the Reform movement of the nineteenth century, which also was a major influence on Conservative Judaism.

In the kitchen today, being served is an old man named Raphael. Born in Drohobycz, he came from a poor family. He speaks French, Polish, Russian, Yiddish, English, and Hebrew. In 1926 he went to France to study to be a dentist. The war turned him into a member of the French Resistance. He stayed in France until 1950, marrying a Frenchwoman and becoming a French citizen. He became a dentist at last, then became interested in sports medicine.

He returned to Wroclaw and was sent by the Polish government to Moscow, to study gymnastics so he could become a coach. On his return to Wroclaw he worked in a military hospital. By 1960, he had become blind in one eye. Today he spends most of his time reading and writing, and eating his free lunch each day where once a great faculty taught.

It is Sunday and Juzek, son of Genia Lis, plans a trip to what had been the famous Breslau Seminary. Genia has owned her home since 1946, when she came to Wroclaw from the Soviet Union. Juzek, with his Catholic wife Chana and his daughter Ewa, lives upstairs.

Juzek waves goodbye to his family and, for the first time in many years, sets out for the remains of the historic seminary and synagogue.

On arrival, he walks through all the levels, a dangerous trek because of weakened support beams for the staircases. He climbs among the rubble, dirt, papers, broken glass, human feces, and shoes.

Dzierzoniow

Mojzecz Jakubowicz is president of Dzieroniow's Jewish club.

He walks, on a mild sunny day, through the downtown area, passing the Jewish gymnasium, in use until 1968, and the synagogue, built in 1857 and used until 1980. Today the Polish government is paying for its restoration.

Mojzecz, familiarly known as Moshe, was born sixty-five years ago in a small shtetl near Krakow. He was one of nine children. His father worked in a whiskey factory owned by a Jew named Englander. Moshe was sent to a Polish school, then to a trade school. He was taught to make furniture and tapestries.

By 1940, his mothers and sisters all had perished in the Belzec concentration camp. He and the rest of the males of his family survived. He was decorated while serving in the Polish Army; one brother, a furniture maker, survived the war and lived in the nearby town of Bielsk Biermawa; another achieved a high rank in the Soviet Army and survived in Moscow until 1964; even his father survived the Nazis, living until 1953 in Dzierzoniow, where he died at the age of seventy-seven.

Moshe watched the deterioration of the kehilla in Dzierzoniow, after coming to the city in 1946. He worked with 400 other Jews in the textile factory, the main industry of the city. At that time, there were 24,000 Jews in Dzierzoniow, Wroclaw, Bielawa, and Legnica. There were sixteen Jewish cooperatives active in the city itself, and Moshe was involved in them. But the last of the cooperatives was closed in 1949.

Still, after the war, life was not bad in Dzierzoniow. The Jewish cultural organization was officially founded on June 17, 1945. The American Joint Distribution Committee and the Polish government gave money to Jews for resettlement. A Jewish high school was founded, along with a theater and synagogues.

Then came 1968 and student-worker unrest in Poland. The Polish government blamed the Jews for its problems and encouraged emigration to Israel. Moshe believes that this was with the approval of the United States. Whatever the truth of the matter, the result was a disastrous decline in the vitality of the kehilla.

But Moshe keeps the kehilla in his own life. He has two daughters. One, a statistician, lives in Walbrzych; the other lives in Bielawa and works at a bank. Both read, write, and speak Yiddish. Moshe, faithful to his tradition, spends his days organizing people to get money for the disabled, the poor, the orphans, and the sick.

People do not stay strangers long to Moshe. After a few hours he tells anyone he meets: "Mir zaynen fun dem zelbekhe mishpokhe" [We are from the same family]. No one is ill at ease for long.

Another Moshe, Moshe Joseph Goldman, comes to the Jewish club each day from his hometown of Bielawa, seven kilometers from Dzierzoniow.

Born in 1905, he lived through the terrible years of the Holocaust. But Moshe was one the lucky ones. He escaped the Nazis, running to the city of Pinsk. He did not have the proper papers, and the Russian authorities sent him to a work camp in the Karelia region, bordering on Finland. He spent fifteen months in the camp, suffering an injury to his foot.

After a total of six years in the U.S.S.R., in 1946 he returned to Bielawa, where for years he worked in a grocery store.

At eighty, travelling the seven kilometers daily from Bielawa to Dzierzoniow, he sits in the friendly Jewish club and he talks freely.

walbrzych

Chana Najbaum lives in Wroclaw, but has come to Walbrzych to visit a friend, Freyda Schneider, and to enjoy the beauty and charm of this city. Located in the low Carpathian Mountains, near the border with Czechoslovakia, it is more comfortably cooler than surrounding areas, with narrow cobblestone streets and old buildings on hilly terrain.

Chana has been a psychologist for thirty years. Her children, a daughter and a son, live in the United States.

Her family was poor, her father a tailor from Lublin. Her mother had twelve children, of which three women, including Chana, survive. Chana endured the war, working in the forests of Kaminsk-Ulrask in the Urals, then resettling in Poland. Her husband served during the war in the Polish Army and is now a lawyer.

Chana is a strong Communist.

Leib Meyer, Chana's friend, and Freyda's brother, has respect for Jewish tradition. He helps old Jews in the city travel to shul. But he is an atheist, and rarely goes to shul on his own. He appreciates Jewish history, though, and enjoys maintaining some of the rituals.

Today there is a minyan of fifteen. The sanctuary is *not* pleasantly cool, it is frigid. The room, cordoned off for the service, is barely tolerable. But the celebrants carry on.

Leib introduces his visitors to the shul to Ludwig "Eleizer ben Natan" Hoffman, secretary of the Jewish club. Ludwig was born in Drohobycz. In 1942, he was deported to the Gross-Rosen camp, where he was held for the duration of the war. Then he was brought to Walbrzych to work in the large textile factory. He has since watched Jewish life decline. The Jewish collective farms were closed in 1948, the Jewish theater was closed in 1965, and the Jewish schools closed in 1968.

Today there are a hundred Jews in the city; sixty to seventy of them participate in the club. Some of the Jews are members of a mixed marriage. Within nearly all the families, a remnant of Jewish identity is preserved: Shabbat candles are lit; Hebrew or Yiddish folk songs are sung; there are Jewish books and artwork. Some lucky children have grandparents living in their homes.

But in Walbrzych, as in Poland generally, Jews have a low birth rate. Today there are only fifteen young Jews living in Walbrzych. Several of them are unmarried women.

czechoslovakia

pRaGue

It is Shabbat morning at the Jerusalem shul. Mrs. Waltraut Stecher and her son Denny are praying.

Mrs. Stecher, born in a village named Mezholezy, near the Austrian border, lost her family during World War II. But she was hidden by German peasants in what is now East Germany.

Forced to live in a cellar from October 1939 until the beginning of 1946, she made her living as a coal miner. Though she was not threatened, her living and working conditions did bring her tuberculosis.

Nevertheless, she bore Denny in 1940, and both survived to come to Prague after the war's nightmare closed.

In the tenth century Jewish merchants plied the trade routes from the Rhineland to the Near East. By 906 there was a settlement in Bohemia, and by 1091 a permanent kehilla in Prague, its capital.

In 1096 the First Crusade pillaged and killed many Jews, and forced others to be baptized. In 1142, the Second Crusade drove the Jews out of the city.

But they returned, settling on the right bank of the Moldau River in what became Prague's future Jewish quarter. Throughout the twelfth and thirteenth centuries, Jews settled throughout Bohemia, into Moravia, and further east into Slovakia.

In 1270, in the Jewish quarter of Prague, the Alte-Neue Shul (Old-New Synagogue) was built. It is the oldest shul still in use in Europe, and a minyan prays there every day. The kehilla offices, rabbi's study, community archives, and dining hall are all contained, even now, in an early seventeenth century building next to the shul.

By 1600, despite the tribulations, the Jewish community in Prague numbered 2,000. A Jewish Golden Age began, which lasted into the eighteenth century. Synagogues were built, a Hebrew printing house was started, and Jewish craft guilds added splendor to the vibrant kehilla. Prague became a major center of European Jewish life and the home of scholars.

Meanwhile, Bohemia, Moravia, and Silesia became part of Austria, linking the history of Prague's Jews with that of Austria.

One of the age's most vibrant personalities was Rabbi Judah Loew ben Bezalel (c. 1525-1609). He was known not only for rabbinic scholarship, but for his work in secular sciences, particularly mathematics. As Chief Rabbi of Prague, he was the subject of many legends, including that of the Golem.

Rabbi Loew is said to have constructed a clay figure, which he brought to life with the help of God. The Golem was to be his servant and defend the Jews from their persecutors, but it ran amok. Finally, the rabbi had to destroy his creation by removing the magic name from underneath its tongue.

Austrian Emperor Joseph II ruled from 1780 to 1790. He abolished many of the limitations imposed on the Jews. But he also forced them to adopt family names, establish secular schools, and cease using Hebrew and Yiddish in business transactions.

Jews also became subject to military conscription. Some wealthy and industrious Jews took advantage of Joseph's reforms to plunge into manufacturing enterprises, which led to resettlement outside the Jewish ghetto. By 1818, the kehilla's population had grown to 10,000.

In 1867 Jews achieved full legal emancipation. Almost at once secularization and assimilation began.

Jews themselves introduced many reforms to synagogue services, shortening the liturgy, using less Hebrew and more German, and introducing the organ and the mixed choir.

Jews were adopting German language and culture as their own, becoming a considerable part of the German minority of Prague.

As the nineteenth century came to a close, Prague was one of the leading centers of German Jewish literary and intellectual activity, rivaling Berlin and Vienna. Among others, Franz Kafka, Max Brod, and Oskar Baum made monumental reputations while living and writing in Prague.

By 1900, 44.4 percent of Prague's Jews declared themselves to be German. This inflamed anti-Semitism among Czechs. Jews were looked upon as purveyors of Germanization.

Until 1935, Czech grumbling did not endanger the Jews' peaceful existence in Prague. Then began a constant surge of refugees, first from Germany, then from Austria and the Sudentenland, which swelled the kehilla to 56,000 by 1939, when the Nazi occupation began.

Quickly, prominent Jews were arrested and deported from Prague to Buchenwald. Until emigration was halted in October 1941, half of the kehilla fled the growing Nazi terror, many escaping to Palestine.

From October 6, 1941 to March 16, 1945, 46,067 Jews were sent from Prague to Thereseinstadt (Terezin) or other concentration camps.

When the Holocaust was over 10,000 Jews returned to the city. Community life also returned and began to solidify. But the 1948 Communist takeover marked another turning point.

The first formal blow against the Jews was the anti-Semitic trial of Rudolf Slansky, the Jewish Communist First Secretary, in 1952. Purges followed, during which eleven Jews were accused of being "Zionist agents." Jewish religious and secular activities began to stagnate. There were spurts of emigration to Israel and the West.

From 1965 to 1968, political liberalization under Alexander Dubcek infused the kehilla with new ideas and energy. Then came August 1968, when the Soviet Union removed Dubcek and installed a new repressive regime.

Now the kehilla again is on the rebound, with substantial numbers of Jews freshly committed to their culture and to teaching it to their children. This renewal, five years old, has been spurred by Rabbi Daniel Meyer, Czechoslovakia's first new rabbi since 1964. Taught at the rabbinical seminary in Budapest, he remains the only Rabbi in the country. He has instilled hope in young adults that their children might be taught Hebrew and the ways and tradition of Judaism.

One of these young adults is Denny Stecher. His son has been bar mitzvahed and his daughter trained in Jewish history and traditions. Stecher keeps a traditional Jewish home.

This year's celebration of Hanukkah is a merry one. There is a lavish party of food, drink, dancing, singing, storytelling, and clowns for the kehilla's children. Eighty children, accompanied by parents and grandparents, attend the lighting of the menorah. The next evening, the adults attend the solemn study of the customs and laws given reverence again during Hanukkah. In his office, the rabbi repeated the serious lessons so crucial to the Jews' endurance. On the fifth night, the adults play as the children had. There is a kosher meal, a choral concert, and hearty revelry—including dancing to a New Orleans jazz band.

After the Holocaust, 25,000 Jews remained of the 375,000 who had lived in Czechoslovakia before World War II. Now only 7,000 are registered as Jews, with another 3,000 unregistered, many of them married to non-Jews.

In Trnava, Bratislava, and Kosice, the kehillot are composed primarily of older Jews.

In the oldest Jewish cemetery in Prague's old Jewish quarter the dead were buried layer upon layer because of lack of space over the years. The decaying coffins have caused the ground to sink and the headstones to shift. And today they lean every which way, at many different angles.

Today young people from Trnava, Bratislava, and Kosice are moving to Prague. This migration, which may doom the other towns and cities to a future without Jews, is bringing fresh hope to the Prague kehilla.

Rabbi Daniel Meyer, Denny Stecher, and the children of Denny Stecher bring fresh hope as well.

KOSICE

An eighty-year-old kitchen in the courtyard of the synagogue of Kosice serves lunch to Jews and non-Jews alike. It is Saturday and, as always on that day, tcholent and potato kugel, traditional Shabbat fare, are being served. As they eat, the Jews tell vibrant stories of the rich Jewish life in Kosice before the Holocaust.

Kosice (Hungarian, Kassa; German, Kaschau) lies in southeast Slovakia, in the Carpatho-Russia area. In the eighteenth century, Hasidic émigrés from Galicia invigorated the Carpatho-Russia cities of Munkác (Mukacevo), Uzhgorod (Ungvar), and Hurzt with a lively piety centered around their particular tzaddikim. Hundreds of pogroms in Tsarist Russia forced another wave of Hasidim to this area in 1881. Orthodox and Hasidic living styles, therefore, dominated eastern parts of Czechoslovakia, and continued to do so until the beginning of World War II.

Hungarian Jews attended the fairs of Kosice as early as the eighteenth century. In 1840 some of these Jewish merchants gained permission to settle in the city, leading to a kehilla of thirty-two families.

In 1843, these people built a synagogue, which still is in use. But today it is a repository for technical books, having been leased to the State by the kehilla after the war.

As for the kehilla, it began to flourish in 1860. The city gained importance as a railroad junction for commerce traveling south to Budapest, north to Krakow. Jews founded a brewery, flour mills, a soap factory, and a pulp mill—much of the lifeblood of the city's industry.

By 1869, a schism had developed. There were two distinct kehillot, a small one of Orthodox Jews and a large one of Liberal Jews. The latter drew most of its support from the Hungarian Jews of Kosice.

An Hungarian hegemony burgeoned through the years within the Kosice Jewish community. The young in Jewish elementary schools were taught in Hungarian. Consequently, Czechs saw the Jews of Carpatho-Russia as the bearers of Magyarization, as the Czechs of Prague had come to distrust the Jews there as bearers of Germanization.

By 1910, fifteen percent of Kosice's population (about 7,000 persons) was Jewish. At the end of World War I, Czechoslovakia was carved out of the Austro-Hungarian Empire, and Kosice swelled with a wave of Jewish refugees. Gateway to Carpatho-Russia, the city drew Jews from remote rural areas who sought a better social and economic environment. The kehilla became an eclectic mix—wealthy Hungarian Jews, middle-class Slovakian Jews, and rural Carpatho-Russian Jews.

In 1927 a liberal synagogue was built (which still stands). By 1935, 12,000 Jews were living in Kosice.

On November 2, 1938, Hungary annexed Kosice and sanctions against Jewish businesses began at once. Despite that, refugees from Poland and rural Slovakia rushed to the city—only to become part of the entrapped.

Beginning in 1940, all Jewish men between the ages of forty and forty-five were conscripted into forced-labor battalions to serve in the Ukraine. Deportations to the extermination camps were delayed until 1944, but when they came they came with a vengeance. Only 300 Kosice Jews survived the war—many of those having been interred in Hungarian labor camps.

After the war, the kehillot of eastern Czechoslovakia were renewed with money from the government and from the American Jewish Joint Distribution Committee.

Two rabbis, both graduates of the Kosice Yeshiva, re-introduced shekhita (ritual slaughter), the mikvah, and religious worship. Maccabi sport clubs and music clubs played again. Even Zionist training farms were established, by the Hashomer Ha-Tzair.

But traditional anti-Semitic activities by the peasant population in and around Kosice were also resurrected. As a result, more than a thousand Jews left the city in 1949 and 1950, going to Israel.

The deterioration of the kehilla continued. Today there are only 260 registered Jews in the kehilla. There are perhaps another 600 Jews not affiliated with the kehilla and registered as Slovaks.

But there is strong life still surging in the kehilla. And, as with the Jewish lunch, it is centered in the synagogue courtyard. The atmosphere there is Hasidic, as it had been in prewar days, when many followed the Satmar or Mukachevor rebbes. The melodies of prayers are Hasidic melodies. The kehilla religious leader, shokhet Shimson Grossman, still wears the special Shabbat kaftan of the Hasidim.

The shamash of the synagogue, Benjamin, lost a wife and two children to Auschwitz. But after the war he remarried and the marriage produced a son, now a mechanic.

As he has for twelve years, Benjamin lives in the synagogue courtyard. He shares the traditional Shabbat Saturday lunch of tcholent and potato kugel. He also shares the stories.

BRatislava

The body of a dead old woman is carried, on a wooden stretcher, by close friends, from the hadar-tahorah (purification room) into the snow and ice of the Bratislava winter. During her funeral service, moments before, the men had stood separately from the women.

The body is clad in a shroud. A traditional black velvet burial mantle, inscribed with the names of the founding members of the hevra kedisha (burial society), covers the shroud. The path to the hill of gravestones is narrow and blown by wet snow. The sky is slate and the air frigid.

Naphtali Blau, the shamash, stares away from the moving ritual. He had been a close friend of the dead woman. A handful of old men and women hover and shiver by the grave, whispering in Yiddish.

The moment comes and Naphtali climbs down into the grave to receive the body. Since the woman is to be buried only in the shroud, Naphtali uncovers her head. Then he covers her eyelids with shards. And last, a small pouch of dirt from the Holy Land is sprinkled on the grave.

The Jews of Bratislava (Pressburg in German) always have lived on the edge of exile. In 1360 they were expelled, but returned in 1367. The Hungarian government, which ruled the city, twice canceled all outstanding debts owed Jews—in 1441 and 1450. In 1526 came a long diaspora. The Jews were thrown out of the city and not allowed to return until the late seventeenth century.

Jews returned to Bratislava after their exile, though in dangerously small numbers—only 772 by 1736. They came to live in Schlossberg (Castle Hill), an area overlooking the Danube. It became a ghetto in which the Jews were forced to live until 1850. But eighteenth century Jews made the ghetto a center of industry, making the city itself a textile industry leader and an important center of Orthodox learning. The Pressburger Yeshiva—founded in the pre-exile days of the fifteenth century—became a major institution of Jewish learning, with 400 students at its zenith. During this time the city itself became the young focal point of Central European Jewish thought.

In the last days of the eighteenth century a schism began ripping the kehilla. It began under the influence of the Haskalah (Enlightenment) movement, which had developed in Germany. The traditional Orthodox way of life suffered a buffeting that would last more than a century and a quarter.

The ultra-Orthodox kehilla became controversial as a diligent opponent to Zionism. It served as the center of the Agudat Israel of Czechoslovakia. The Hungarian Zionist Organization was founded in 1902 in Bratislava. In 1904, the World Mizrachi Organization was founded. The Zionist activists of Bratislava united in 1928.

The kehilla, though, remained vibrant. Between the end of the First World War and the beginning of the Second, Bratislava supported twenty synagogues and maintained substantial educational, charitable, and social institutions. The city grew into a significant Hebrew and Yiddish center, producing 340 books between 1831 and 1930. The Jewish population grew to twelve percent of the total population (15,000 persons). During this period, another 5,600 persons were registered as Jewish Slovaks.

But the kehilla's social health and intellectual power were no match for the anti-Semitic terror.

Inspired by the Kristalnacht pogroms in Germany and Austria on November 9 and 10, 1938, attacks gutted Bratislava's Jewish businesses, synagogues, and yeshivas beginning on November 11—exactly twenty years after the end of the "war to end all wars." The expelling of 1,000 Jewish university students, restrictions on all Jews, and pogroms all followed.

Nevertheless, as refugees from Poland and rural Slovakia had fled to Kosice only to be trapped, so did refugees from Vienna flee to Bratislava—mostly to be trapped. The wish was to flee to Palestine (illegally) aboard transports beginning their journeys in Bratislava.

Many, those of the kehilla and those who fled to it with hope, either were deported to the nearby camps of Patronka and Petrzalka—and killed there—or sent to Theresienstadt, then to Auschwitz and other death camps.

After the war, few Jews returned to Bratislava. On the other hand, by 1946, Bratislava had become the headquarters for all the reestablished kehillot of Slovakia. But many of the young Jews were strongly Zionist and belonged to the Hashomer Ha-Tzair movement. As their brothers did in Kosice they prepared for the destiny they had chosen for themselves—aliya to Israel—by building training farms. And, in 1949, 4,000 Jews departed the kehilla for Israel. They received the help of both the Czechoslovakian and Israeli governments.

Now there are only 700 or 800 Jews in Bratislava, of which 200 are unregistered, participating in the kehilla only occasionally. Another 200 or 300 have chosen to register as Slovaks rather than as Jews. All that remains of the ghetto is a single, long-abandoned building with the street sign "Zidovska Ulica" (Jewish Street).

Nevertheless, sixty-five-year-old shamash Naphtali—who has said goodbye to his old friend in her grave—holds a minyan in the only synagogue still open. Born in Kosice (in the village of Stropka), the shamash has worked all his life as a laborer. This, along with his piety, has made him a thinker and, thinking of the thousands who have died in

"Do you see that cement square in the backyard of the synagogue with those metal rods that form a frame? This is for a khupah. The last time we used it was five years ago; now it stands in the snow bare and rusted."

The seventy-five-year-old leader of the Yiddish club of Bratislava, Arye Dojc is an historian. Once he was the principal of a vocational high school. He has a son, thirty-eight, who left for Toronto in 1969. He has a daughter, thirty-five, who left for Israel in 1970 and is now a Jerusalem pharmacist. His two brothers had fled before the war, finally to live in Israel. His sister had survived three years in Auschwitz, also to live in Israel.

Of his hometown, Michalovce, he knows that there had been 5,000 Jews there before the war, 400 just as the war ended, forty

Of his hometown, Michalovce, he knows that there had been 5,000 Jews there before the war, 400 just as the war ended, forty today. He had taught Hebrew there. Of the 740 children of his school at the beginning of the deportations in 1944, at the end of the deportations there were 140.

Arye escaped during the war to join the partisans and married a high school math and physics teacher. Now he is one of the elderly ones. The only time young Jews meet the elderly Jews of the kehilla is on the High Holidays, Purim, or Hanukkah.

As an historian, he is devoted to photographing Jewish cemeteries throughout Czechoslovakia. He has visited 200 sites and has photographed gravestones and mausoleums of revered rabbis. He also has lists of old stone monuments and has saved thousands of words written on them.

He also has a list of nearly 1,000 graves destroyed when a road and tunnel were constructed in Bratislava after the Holocaust was ended.

Now the kehilla of Bratislava is small and its existence is characterized by funerals.

hungary

budapest

The dining table of Bela Hap—known to his friends as Ephraim—is prepared as an operating table. A doctor has come from London to perform the brit, the sacred circumcision, on Ephraim.

At forty-one, the doctor says, Ephraim is a youngster compared to the sixty-seven-year-old he had once circumcised. Ephraim is married and has two boys, ten and nine. Though his mother was Jewish, she had been baptized and chose to run an assimilated home during the hard years following the Nazi terror. As a boy and young man, Ephraim had learned a little Yiddishkeit from his grandmother. But his great-grandfather had been a Ba'al Tefila, a shokhet, and hazzan in his shtetl at the turn of the century.

Ephraim now turns to his great-grandfather's photograph on the wall, lies on the dining room table, and accepts the doctor's medicine and the knife that joins him to his ancestors.

Excited at this passage of a sacred rite, Ephraim soon rises from the table and briefly, feverishly celebrates, giving his friends wine, cake, and cold cuts. Then he sleeps a while, later inviting neighbors and friends to fill his house with Jewish dance and food.

This day was the fulfillment of a journey consciously taken by Ephraim and his wife Chana, a journey that began in the reform movement in Hungary (which during their lifetime had grown strong as one way to keep the kehillot alive), then became mired in day-to-day life. But stirrings and a sense of loss grew, and they chose pietistic friends, joining the Satmar Hasidim that had emigrated to Antwerp, Belgium. Ephraim and Chana talked, then chose to live a traditional Jewish life.

They chose to observe the Shabbat, send the boys to Hebrew school, eat with yarmulkes on their heads, pray twice daily, and eat the beautiful Shabbat meal of challah, tcholent, kugel, matzoh ball soup, and the pleasureable Shabbat desserts. At the evening meal, the sons are tested on the Torah lessons of the week.

And now Ephraim bears on his body his Jewishness.

Budapest has perhaps the most vibrant kehilla in Eastern Europe. There are an Orthodox day school, a Hebrew high school, kosher kitchens, Jewish museums, a mikvah (ritual bath), synagogues (Orthodox, Neolog and Status Quo), a kosher winery, butcher shops, and a kosher bakery. The city also has the only seminary in all of Eastern Europe that has served constantly since 1877, teaching rabbinical and cantorial lessons. All this allows young but maturing families, such as Ephraim's, to thrive.

The earliest Jews in the region followed the footsteps of the Roman legions. Under later Magyar rulers, Jews from Germany, Bohemia, and Moravia were welcomed as they settled up and down the Danube River Valley.

The Jews showed a talent for commerce. Talent bred a strong community, and a strong community bred fear and distrust. By the eleventh century, the first anti-Jewish regulations had been issued. In 1092, the Catholic Church forbad marriage between Jews and Christians, working on Sundays and Christian holidays, and Jewish ownership of Christian slaves. From the twelfth through the fourteenth centuries, decrees tightened the bonds on Jewish life until badges became required—a precursor in red cloth of the Nazis half a millennium later.

Through medieval times, however, the

Jews persisted, establishing thirty-eight kehillot throughout the country. Sopron and Buda were among the largest. The first medieval synagogue to be unearthed in Europe was found in Sopron. It was used from 1350 to 1526, when the Turks overran Hungary. Another synagogue, built in 1366 and unearthed in 1966, was found in Buda. It also fell during the time of the Turks.

When the Turks came, in 1526, they deported Jews to Ottoman territory. But two years later the Jews were back in Buda, building a peaceful, prosperous community that would go on unimpeded for 150 years, based on finance, commerce and certain hand crafts. The kehilla grew to more than a thousand by 1660, and was the wealthiest and largest in Hungary. In 1686, the Jews sided with the Turks during the siege of Buda, and the invading Austrians took the city and ended Jewish prosperity.

Then came the resulting expulsions, murders, and ransomings. Hostility from townspeople led the Jews to live in villages. But as shopkeepers, peddlers, and artisans they had enough success to have to pay "Malke geld" (queen money), to Maria Theresa (1740-1780) as a "tolerance tax." Her son, Joseph II (1780-1790) improved conditions for the kehilla, abolishing special taxes and permitting Jews to settle in royal cities. Throughout this period the Jewish population swelled, because of natural increase and immigration, to more than 500,000. Nevertheless, life for Jews under the Austrian Hapsburgs was always unstable, until Hungary became an independent kingdom in 1867.

During the sixty years or so before World War I, the Pest kehilla grew culturally and economically. The three most famous synagogues of Pest, all in use today, were built: the Moorish-style Reform Dohàny Temple, in 1859; the octagonal Conservative Rombach Temple, in 1872; the Orthodox Kazinczy Synagogue, in 1913. Also established were the Rabbinical Seminary—the only one remaining in Eastern Europe today—and its Jewish youth secondary school, in 1877. This youth school now is known as the Anne Frank Gymnasium.

After the Great War, a short-lived Communist government, led by Bela Kun, a Jew, failed before the onslaught of fascist regent Admiral Miklos Horthy. Anti-Semitism subsided, only to re-emerge. From 1938 to 1941 anti-Jewish laws invaded the lives of 725,000 Jews of Greater Hungary.

Then came the Nazis on March 19, 1944. Seventy percent of the Jews in the countryside were deported to Auschwitz. Jews in urban areas were prodded into the Budapest Ghetto, where 40,000 perished at the hands of the Nazis and Hungarian Arrow Cross soldiers. By the war's end, 450,000 Hungarian Jews had perished.

Budapest held 80,000 to 90,000 Jews at that time. There were glimmerings of hope within a decade, culminating in the anti-Communist rebellion of 1956, which was crushed by Soviet tanks. 25,000 Jews left Budapest to emigrate West.

As the Jewish population declined, the life remained strong enough to support one synagogue, a Talmud Torah school, and a rabbi in each of the eighteen administrative districts of the city. Until its closing in 1980, the Orthodox kehilla maintained a yeshiva at the Kazinczy synagogue. Immigration to Israel, the United States, and Belgium took many young Orthodox Jews. The famed Rabbinical Seminary today has six students on a full-time basis.

It is Sunday. Ephraim takes his sons Ignace and Abraham on the subway to Buda to services at the Leo Frankel synagogue. The boys are joined by many others. Then comes an hour of Hebrew classes for those who do not know the language. They learn to read and write, and rabbinical students teach them how to put on tefilin. The boys study hard, and laugh as boys laugh.

The Dohàny Synagogue, largest in all Europe, seating more than 3,000, has an organ of 5,000 pipes. Franz Liszt and Camille Saint-Saëns played compositions on it. Once

31

the Nazis had surrounded it with a wooden fence, creating the Budapest Ghetto. Today it is the focal point of the fortieth anniversary of the city's liberation from the Nazis by the Soviets.

The city's chief rabbi speaks as the yartzeit candles burn. The older ones cry into the cold gray day. It is a somber hour. Behind the rabbi, on the memorial, flowers are placed by chilled, sturdy hands, signalling the survival of the kehilla.

The kosher kitchen known as the "Hannah" is run by the Orthodox kehilla. A meal costs about four dollars and American tourists come here. The seminary's kosher kitchen is frequented by younger and older Jews. Here a meal is forty cents, and there is talk with teachers and students.

Moshe Yehudah Kovari's kosher butcher shop is the only privately owned one in all of Hungary. The shop is cold as a freezer. His wife works with him.

Gabi sells chickens and wine for the kehilla. The kosher wine cellar is not far from the Kacinczy shul. In the hall outside the cellar, people are drinking. They are gentiles who have come to see Gabi because they know the wine is not watered down. Enthusiastically, they drink of the Jewish life.

It is a weekday lunchtime at heder in the city. Before the meal, the children sing their songs at the tops of their lungs. Then there is soup, meat, potatoes, hot vegetables, bread, and juice or water. After grace, the youngest of the children, two to four, nap in another room, their beds in a careful line. The heder is clean, having been refurbished in 1982 by money from the American Joint Distribution Committee.

Children here learn how to read and write Hebrew, how to speak it. The children study the holidays and the Torah. And they sing. Their parents, people like Ephraim and Chana who have chosen to live the history, pay thirty cents each day for this teaching. The parents know how important the teaching is.

The children only know it is a pleasure to grow up Jewish.

pomaz and vac

Pomaz, twenty kilometers from Budapest, is a small town. Rabbi Itzkhak Goldberg, born in Budapest and taken by his parents to America, has come to Pomaz to find Jewish books, glassware, silver, and other treasures of the tradition. As many Satmar Hasidim, he has come most of all to visit the graves of the great Satmar rabbis. He has come to see the cemeteries, the omnipresent symbol of the kehillot of Eastern Europe, characterizing Pomaz as it does Budapest—and Prague and Warsaw as well.

The former mayor of Pomaz, from 1963 to 1980, Istvan Boross, is also a collector of Jewish memorabilia. He and Rabbi Goldberg speak of Jewish history and tradition.

In 1740, the first Jews, from Moravia, arrived to work as merchants and artisans. In 1820, they were granted a site for a cemetery, and built their first synagogue shortly thereafter. In 1892, Mr. Boross's grandfather donated the land for a second synagogue.

Before the Holocaust, 1300 Jews lived in Pomaz. At its end, only 300 had survived.

Today there is no synagogue nor any kehilla office. Only five Jewish families reside in the town.

Two weeks later Mr. Boross takes friends on a drive to the small companion town of Vac. First they go to the ruins of the synagogue. The last shul in Vac, it has not been used since the war. Today it has only one sign of its Jewish past: a Magen David on its top. Inside, the vaulted ceilings reveal hints of what had once been beautiful paintings. It has rained the night before, and the visitors stride through mud—even within the ruin.

Jews had come through Vac in the seventeenth and eighteenth centuries on the trade route from Vienna to Budapest, on the Danube River. The kehilla formally began in 1841, and the first synagogue was built in 1864, becoming the Status Quo synagogue in 1869, serving craftsmen and contractors.

By the 1930s, there were more than 3,000 Jews in Vac. The kehilla supported the original synagogue, and Orthodox one built in 1882, a yeshiva, a middle school, two elementary schools, and one Talmud Torah.

Then came the Nazis. Jews were herded in the ghetto in Budapest in July 1944, then deported to Auschwitz. Three hundred Jews returned to Vac after the war.

The Hungarian peasantry accused the Jews of siding with the Soviets during the failed revolution of 1956. Many Jews fled the kehilla to go to Budapest and other urban areas. Now there are fifteen Jews. There is no synagogue, and there is a minyan only on Rosh Hashana and Yom Kippur. These services are held in the home of Jozsef and Caroline Samuel.

Once rosh kahal of Vac, Jozsef talks energetically in Yiddish, punctuating his talk with jokes. Today he talks with Mr. Boross and his friends, who have capped their trip to Vac with a visit to his house, the house of a man who has worked with his hands all his life and has lived and breathed Jewish history. He admits that he must borrow a Torah from Budapest each year for the High Holidays. Then he laughs and says "Okay. Now let's have some schnapps to celebrate."

Next, Jozsef tells his own story: He was born in Szendehely, a village near Vac. His father made an Orthodox home, and ran a small inn where Jozsef played the trumpet. Jozsef fought in both the Great War and World War II, and was sent to the labor camp of Verbo for two and one-half years during the Second World War. His mother and two sisters died in Auschwitz. He speaks Yiddish and Hungarian in his traditional home, which he has created with Caroline, who was born in the small village of Steidorf in Romania.

She willingly chose the traditional life and has stayed with it for the fifty-four years of her married life with Jozsef.

Jozsef turns to his friends who have visited from Pomaz, and laments that the Jews of Vac are assimilated and ashamed to admit their Jewishness. For himself, he says: "I am a Jew. I am not ashamed to remain a Jew."

miskolc

Two Hungarian gypsies, a boy eighteen, and his brother fifteen, are playing guitars on the train to Miskolc. As the riders on the train listen to the lively gypsy music, they can see the mountains of northeastern Hungary become the puszta—steppes—of the eastern region.

The first Jewish settlers who saw these steppes and made their homes there made their money selling alcoholic beverages. Liberal municipal laws allowed them to own houses and land and operate their own judiciary, and the kehilla imposed fines and corporal punishment.

From the beginning of the nineteenth century until the time of the Nazis, Jews made up twenty percent of Miskolc's population—the largest percentage of any city in Hungary.

They centered their community on their cemetery, opened in 1759, which still is used. They built their first synagogue in 1765, and built their Great Synagogue in 1861—which still is in use. They also succumbed to the ideological schism that raged in all the Jewish communities of Eastern Europe as the Haskala (Enlightenment) movement became powerful in the 1870s. Violent confrontations between Orthodox and liberal Neolog Jews followed, leading to separate kehillot in 1875.

As elsewhere, the internal conflict led to temporary vitality. At the beginning of the twentieth century, the kehillot maintained three yeshivot, an elementary school, two middle schools, the only seminary for female teachers in Hungary, and a traditional Jewish religious school operated by the Satmar Hasidim. As the Nazis approached, there were 12,000 Jews in the community.

Hungary joined Germany in invading Russia on June 22, 1941, and this was the beginning of the systematic persecution of Jews in Miskolc. Youth and the elderly alike were conscripted into labor battalions. They were taken to occupied Ruthenia and the Ukrainian front, where most were exterminated. Germans occupied Hungary on March 19, 1944, beginning the exportation of all Jews to Auschwitz. One hundred five eventually returned. When the war ended, Miskolc became a center for Jews returning from concentration camps, swelling the kehilla to 2,353 members in 1946.

Lipot Klein, the rosh kahal, is one of the 400 Jews in Miskolc today, and the father of Gabi, the wine-seller of Budapest. He attends the synagogue twice every day. Today he eats lunch at the kosher kitchen, in the courtyard of the monolithic Great Synagogue. He is one of the old ones who partake of the Jewish life centered here, where there are also the kosher butcher shop, kehilla offices, the shokhet's workshop, and Beit Midrash. Today the butcher shop is open. Shekhita has taken place.

One of the shul members finishes the meal, waves goodbye to Lipot and the others, and walks to a private home. It is the home of Chaya Preicz and her husband. She has come from a traditional home, and is a quick, happy woman, who speaks in excited Yiddish. As those inside the brick wall, she and her husband live a traditional life, keep a traditional Jewish home.

nyiregyhaza and nagykallo

Elizabeth and Magdalena György are shouting call numbers into a CB (citizen's band) radio, then yelling "breaker, breaker" after their messages. They are trying to call Elizabeth's son Andras (who wants to be known as "Andrew") to lunch. The lunch is good and hot, in a clean, modern, lively home. Elizabeth, seventy-eight, calls Andras in English, French, or Yiddish, when the Hungarian fails. Magda, seventy-four, a little quieter, a little more patient, simply waits for Andras to return.

But Andras doesn't answer. He has taken three friends to the neighboring town of Nagykallo to visit the cemetery. They are seeking the grave of the revered Reb Kallo.

These four young men drive to the local pub. They must get the key to the cemetery from the gentile who keeps it. They get the key, but the key doesn't fit. Undaunted, they leap the low fence. Once inside, they find five gravestones standing, one with readable Hebrew writing.

They climb up and peer through the grating of the Rebbe's tomb. Graffiti are all over the walls, and there are kvittlakh (little pieces of paper, personal notes) from visitors over the years.

Rebbe Isaac Itzkhak Kallo died in 1821. He was the first Hasidic leader to live permanently in Hungary. On his yartzeit (7 Adar), Hasidim from America, Europe, and Israel come to visit, to be still, to think, and to pay their respects. And now the three young men visit to pay their respects.

Jews lived in the district from the early eighteenth century, but were excluded from the city until 1840. Until the mid-nineteenth century, the kehilla was controlled by Hasidic adherents of Rebbe Itzkhak of Taub, who lived in Nagykallo. But the 1869 general Jewish congress led to power for the liberal and modernist groups, who established a separate kehilla apart from the Orthodox and Hasidic.

Government words emancipated Jews who were Hungarian by nationality, but anti-Semitism filled everyday life. In 1882 court hearings concerning the notorious Tiszaeszlar blood-libel case were held in Nyiregyhaza. Still, Jews prospered economically and socially. There were 3,008 Jews in the kehilla in 1900; 5,134 in 1936.

As the Nazi onslaughts began, Jewish refugees from Poland and Slovakia, assisted by a special communal committee, arrived in the city. Then came March 19, 1944 and German occupation. On April 19, 1944, during Passover, the ghetto was established. Jews herded in from surrounding areas swelled the ghetto to 17,850. Thousands and thousands ended in Auschwitz and Birkenau. After the war, 1300 returned.

Of the three synagogues standing before the war, only the Martirok Synagogue remained afterwards. From this synagogue, the last rabbi of the town, Dr. Bela Bernstein, had led services, then had been deported himself to Auschwitz.

Today, during Shabbat and holidays, services are held in the synagogue. Once each week, Itzhak Weiss, shokhet from Budapest, comes to kosher cows, chickens, and geese. On the days of shekhita (kosher slaughtering), the butcher shop becomes lively with tradition, lively with talk and jokes.

A Hebrew teacher visits from Miskolc by train every other week, but teaches only four or five students. Most Jewish youth have gone to Budapest for the vibrancy of that kehilla and for its cosmopolitan opportunities.

Now there are seventy Jews left in Nyiregyhaza. And two of them are visiting the Jewish cemetery in Nagykallo.

ꝺEBRECEN

It is Shabbat, after services, and the squeals and laughter of twenty-five children fill the hall leading to the kosher kitchen. The squeals and laughs become ordered into responses to questions about Hebrew and history as these children share the history.

Responses made, some lessons learned, the children are served Shabbat meal of kugel, cholent, chicken soup, and honeycake. The older men of the kehilla have served the children. They will coordinate holiday programs for the young ones.

Their other duties include: maintaining the town's only mikvah, holding the weekly Torah study session, and running the kehilla offices. Debrecen's kehilla is the second largest in Hungary. In the winter its Orthodox synagogue becomes too cold to serve its people, and the smaller one in the courtyard must be used.

Debrecen, in eastern Hungary, did not have an organized kehilla until 1851. Jews had lived in the area since the beginning of the nineteenth century, but not until then did they receive permission to obtain land for a synagogue and cemetery.

The first synagogue (Status Quo) was built in 1885. The second (Orthodox) was built in 1893, after factionalism in 1886 had led the Orthodox to form a separate kehilla.

Despite anti-Semitic disruptions, such as the Tiszaeszlar blood-libel, Jewish population grew from 118 in 1848 to 12,000 in 1940. The then Horthy regime deported many young Jews to labor camps in Ruthenia (Carpatho-Russia, in the Ukraine).

Then came May 1944, when the Germans rounded up Jews from surrounding villages and put them into the Debrecen Ghetto. From June 26 to 28, 1944, 7,500 were deported to Auschwitz. The rest had to be taken to Austria, the railway lines having been cut by Allied bombings.

The Jews who survived and chose to return to Debrecen formed a kehilla that by

1947 had become the third largest in Hungary, after Budapest and Szeged.

Sandor Polanauer studied at the seminary in Budapest. In the Budapest kehilla, Sandor and his wife Nora became active—lecturing, attending lectures, singing with other young Jews, keeping the tradition. Sandor became the rabbi of the Reform synagogue in Debrecen in 1983. He strengthened its life, forming a choir, teaching at the Hebrew school. Most of all he provided the young children with a Jewish role model, a man of the tradition to admire and emulate.

Sandor and Nora had a baby boy, and in the summer of 1984 they all left Debrecen to join Sandor's brother, Kfar Habad, in Israel. The void has not yet been filled. Today Satmar Hasid Rov Yidl Weiss of Miskolc is the only rabbi outside of Budapest. The old ones of Debrecen are the only ones left to teach the young children of the few young families.

But there are twenty-five voices in the kitchen after Shabbat services and, for the four hundred members of the kehilla, there is vitality. Shammes Yankel Weiss puts it this way: "Klayn ober nokh a guter leben un fargenign" [Small but still a good and pleasurable life].

ROMANIA

BUCHAREST

Dr. Edith Varga flattens the end of her stethoscope against the back of an old woman and presses the hearing pieces against her ears. She checks for lung congestion, then smiles, finding none. She is serving the residents of the Calea Calarasi Jewish Old Age Home. The woman smiles and relinquishes her place to a man, who raises his shirt for the smiling, easy-going Edith. The doctor is a survivor of Auschwitz.

At this moment, at the Choral Temple, chief synagogue of Bucharest, Israeli Prime Minister Shimon Peres speaks to more than 4,000. The government has placed police guards not only here, but at most major synagogues, the Yiddish theater, and the kosher cantina. The kehilla is tense, lively, and alert on this icy day of winter.

Balkan rabbis have recorded that this kehilla was first made up of Sephardic merchants and moneylenders from Turkey and the Balkan countries. The princess that ruled Walachia, of which Bucharest was capital until Romanian independence in 1878, brought some leading Jews to Bucharest, raising them to positions of power. During the late seventeenth century, Jews from Galicia and the Ukraine fled Chmielnicki and his Cossacks, forming an Ashkenazic core for the city's kehilla.

Life stayed quiet during the eighteenth century. By the beginning of the nineteenth century, however, the Jews had established synagogues and schools, had gained a strong economic presence, and had become a competitive threat. Anti-Semitism grew.

But, the kehilla prospered. By 1860, the Jewish population was 40,533—14.7 percent of the population of the city. Traditional internal conflicts split the Jews into four kehillot: the native Askhenazic, the Austrian and Prussian, the Russian, and the Sephardic. Social welfare and education were attended to by the four groups jointly. But each had its own synagogue and religious leaders. The powerful Choral Temple was built by the wealthy Reform Austrian-Prussian kehilla.

In the late 1870s, in response to the strength of Jewish political activity, King Carol I introduced harsh anti-Jewish laws which forbad Jews from becoming lawyers, chemists, teachers, railway officials, army officers, and pharmacists. This intolerance culminated in 1893 with the expulsion of Jewish students from public schools. Thousands fled to America.

The Versailles Treaty provided for minority rights, theoretically raising the status of Bucharest Jews after World War I. In 1920, the city government made the Ashkenazic community sole legal representative of the kehilla's religious, educational, and welfare institutions, the forty synagogues, two hospitals, two cemeteries, nineteen schools, the library, museum, the clinic, the two old-age homes, and the two orphanages.

The Antonescu-Iron Guard coalition took government control in September 1940, putting the Jews in terror until its overthrow in August 1944. Most cursed was the murderous pogrom of January 21-24, 1941. Iron Guard soldiers marched through Jewish quarters randomly beating and arresting thousands, destroying Jewish businesses, setting fires, pillaging synagogues, and murdering 120 Jews.

The government expropriated the homes of Jews in the outlying towns, swelling the kehilla's number to 100,000. Only 27.2 percent were employed because of work restrictions. The crowding was maddening because the government had taken 15,000 apartments belonging to Jews.

But only a few hundred Bucharest Jews were transported and killed in the camps of Transnistria. Most managed to survive the war.

The Communists took control in 1947, leading to the nationalization of Jewish societies, which finally were organized into the Federation of Jewish Communities of Romania.

Yiddish flourished during the 1950s. A Yiddish school of dramatic art opened, Yiddish theater was popular, and a Yiddish weekly newspaper, *Ikuf Bleter*, was published. The 1960s brought emigration to Israel, and the end of most of these institutions.

The 17,000 Jews of Bucharest today make the community the second-largest concentration of Jews in one city in the Eastern Bloc. Twelve synagogues operate, four with a daily minyan. One hundred students attend the Talmud Torah each Sunday. The young sing and play music for holidays offering special programs for foreign guests.

The snow and ice that clogs the grounds of the Choral Temple and the Calea Calarasi Home also fills the Ashkenazic cemetery. Unlike many of the sad, deformed cemeteries of Eastern Europe, this one is proud and awesome. The Jewish tradition lives powerfully here, epitomized by the Struma Memorial. During the Holocaust, Jewish refugees filled the S.S. Struma seeking sanctuary in Palestine. But Turkish and British authorities would not let the ship pass the Bosphorous Straits because its passengers had no visas for Palestine. Ordered back to the Romanian coast, it sank when it hit a mine. Seven hundred sixty-nine names are inscribed on the memorial.

For the Jews visiting the cemetery, their city is poor, not quite able to keep up with winter; not enough fuel for the stoves, not enough meat and cracers to meet the demand, no fruit but badly bruised cold storage apples.

Still, the very pious Rabbi Marulies walks from the Mare Synagogue to his home in the shul courtyard. Proud and Orthodox through and through, he wears his tefilin and tallit.

At the smaller Tailors' Wives' shul, gypsies shovel away the snow outside. Inside, the shamash has stoked the stove. But only next to the old stove is the temperature bearable.

Chief Rabbi Dr. Moses Rosen eats his lunch this frigid day, as usual, in the large kosher cantina of Bucharest, which is named "Popa Soare." Tourists, a few elderly Jews, and Jewish employees also eat here. At the other kosher cantina, in the courtyard of the Mare Synagogue, all gentiles employed by the kehilla who wish a Jewish meal eat, along with many of the old Jews. The two kitchens share a common atmosphere, which fights the cold as does the food: lively, with a mix of old and young, the voices speaking Romanian, Yiddish, and Hebrew.

Dr. Rosen, a renowned Jewish leader and elected government official, finishes his lunch. He has spoken with a high-ranking world official. A government-chauffeured limousine drives away from the courtyard. In the cold, poor kehilla of Bucharest, this activity is normal.

ðoROhoi

Zipporah is singing in a tight, crying vibrato. The Jewish songs are accompanied by the violin of a young man Zipporah has just met.

The music stops after forty-five minutes. Zipporah tells her new young friend to rest, sit down, and eat something. She has been a bookkeeper all her life and now is a resident of the Old Age Home. Asked of her life from her youth, she replies: "Ikh bin a fruma yidine" [I am an observant Jewess].

Jews began to settle in Dorohoi in the sixteenth century, when that area of northeast Romania was ruled by the Ottoman Empire. The majority at that time were Sephardic, having traveled north from Turkey through Bulgaria on trade routes that led as far north as what is now Lithuania. The Cossack murders followed in the seventeenth century, leading to the Polish-Russian, Ashkenazic majority.

In the nineteenth century Jews enjoyed success as artisans, manual workers, shopkeepers, and farmers. By 1896, the kehilla numbered 7,000, fifty-two percent of the total population. It established its first Talmud Torah and secular schools. Then came World War I, the persecution by government military authorities, and the stubborn endurance of the community. Jewish organizations grew—from the hospital to the sports club.

In 1940, anti-Jewish laws were first promulgated by King Carol II. He was soon replaced by Ion Antonescu and the cruel power of the Iron Guard.

Pogroms followed. Between October 1941 and December 1942, 3,000 Jews from Dorohoi and outlying smaller kehillot were sealed in railroad cars and taken to Transnistria. In April 1944, the Russians took control of Transnistria. Two thousand Jews returned to Dorohoi, under Soviet army control. After the war 6,000 Jews lived in Dorohoi, the city's kehilla having survived in better condition than many.

Twenty-eight synagogues, including shtieblekh (small Orthodox prayer buildings), existed. Today there are four: the Rabinzon, where a minyan meets on Erev Shabbat and Shabbat; the adjacent Beit Solomon and Rindalior synagogues, which alternate twice day minyans every other week; and the Mare Synagogue, which is used only on High Holidays and is being restored with government funds.

There are only 368 Jews in Dorohoi's populations of 22,000. But Yiddish is spoken on the streets. Jews forty and older speak it; those younger speak some and understand more. Kehilla life emanates from the connecting buildings of the kosher kitchen, kehilla offices, and shekhita building. Death,

assimilation, and aliya to Israel has not shaken the special vitality.

One hundred years ago, Jewish farmers built the Rindalior Synagogue. This is a cold Erev Shabbat, and the farmers have come in horse-drawn wagons with their families to celebrate. Even with the changes one hundred years have made, it could be 1925.

It is Purim morning. Rov Wasserman reads the Megillah Esther to a large crowd, which has been drawn to the Beit Midrash of Beit Solomon by the impending ufruf celebration, when a groom will be called to read from the Torah in anticipation of his wedding day. Weddings, of course, represent hope for the kehilla.

The evening before Rov Wasserman had read the Megillah to a lively crowd in the kosher kitchen. Before the reading the group, many of them young, had watched rock-and-roll videos and a film from Israel. The reading ended with Purim songs sung in Hebrew.

On a normal Wednesday the shokhet—Rov Wasserman—koshers chickens with the help of two peasant women. Two other women, Naha and Fani Cojarcaru, visit the kosher kitchen that afternoon and meet two young visitors who play music for them. With traditional generosity, the women invite the visitors to their house. The rooms are small, there is no running water nor electricity. The beds are made of piles of cardboard. The home was built in 1928 and paid for by their mother's dowry.

Family pictures are shown and tasty muffins nearly burned on the bunsen burner—the sisters' stove—are served. Fani produces a dusty bottle of homemade, strong cherry schnapps. The young visitors cough at the strong drink and all four laugh.

Iasi

The kosher kitchen is a kosher cantina in a strong, columned building in 1983. Four young Jews, students, eat their lunch. Since it is near Purim, they are served hamantashen for dessert. They are charged twenty-seven cents each.

The buildings near it are delapidated. But here, after lunch, the students dance and party. The cantina also is the Jewish club. Today, as in recent days, there are many who will rehearse songs for chorus, hear lectures, eat, talk, and just enjoy each other in a pleasant place.

Located in northeastern Romania, Iasi was once the capital of the principality of Moldavia, then under Turkish rule.

Its kehilla is the oldest in Moldavia, as Jews chose to settle there beginning in the second half of the fifteenth century. The choice was appropriate because of its position on the trade route between Poland and Bessarabia. It is served by the Prut River, which leads to the Black Sea.

As did the kehilla of Bucharest, Iasi's turned from being Sephardic to Ashkenazic, transformed by the Polish and Galician refugees from the Chmielnicki massacres of 1648-1649 and the Cossack pogroms of 1650 and 1652.

Guilds ruled the community from 1622 to 1834, led by the chief rabbi. In 1834, the office was abolished, and Jewish associations were structured according to the countries of origin: Russia, Austria, Prussia.

At the beginning of the nineteenth century, Hasidism became potent by the strength of its leaders. One was Abraham Joshua Heschel, of Apta, Poland. These men built Jewish schools. When anti-Semite Vice Mayor A.C. Cuza expelled Jewish students from public schools in 1893, these Hasidic-inspired schools filled the void. Hebrew language and culture classes thrived. Eventually, nine Zionist organizations were created in 1919.

Yiddish theater and music also thrived. In 1876, Abraham Goldfaden began the first Yiddish theater troupe in the world. It presented operettas—at first in taverns—that inspired many young Jews to go on the Yiddish stage. Music's vitality was symbolized by the Sigally and Bughici families of klezmorim, flourishing from the 1870s until the coming of the Nazis.

By the mid-1920s, fed by this cosmopolitan influence, the Jewish population had reached 45,000, 37 percent of the city's population.

Anti-Semitism was aroused, by Jewish cultural and academic growth between the world wars. Soon there were restrictions on Jewish employment and boycotts of Jewish businesses. This led to an economic decline in the Jewish community.

In 1927, a coalition of anti-Semitic associations at the University of Iasi produced the fascist Iron Guard, under the leadership of Cornelius Zilia Codreano, later to become an intimate of Hitler. They terrorized Jews, though they had no official sanction. On September 4, 1940, General Ion Antonescu seized power from King Carol II, became dictator of Romania, and officially proclaimed Iasi the capital of the Iron Guard. There were immediate mass arrests, tortures, extortions, confiscations of property, and murders of Jews.

This was the precursor of the "aktion" conducted by the Nazis and the Iron Guard June 28-29, 1941. German soldiers systematically rounded up 12,000 Jews. Half were shot in the town square, the other half shipped to concentration camps, with only one-third surviving the suffocating train ride. During the entire Holocaust nearly half of Iasi's Jews were murdered. Today, a memorial plaque inscribed in Hebrew and Romanian stands before the mass grave of the 12,000.

Itzkhak Gott visits the memorial some days. But today he leads a rehearsal of the Jewish choir in the kosher cantina. He has taken this choir to Israel and Switzerland and, leading the Bucharest Jewish choir as well, has brought Romanian Jewish music for the first time ever to the United States.

As the musicians rehearse, two synagogues wait for worshippers; they have a minyan each day. Three others stand waiting for

40

Shabbat and another awaits the High Holidays. They serve the 1,500 Jews of the kehilla.

But the strength is in the kosher cantina, where the young—including not only Jewish students of Romania, but medical and dentistry students from Israel—joke with the old. Students from Arabic and African countries do not eat at the cantina, but do attend the universities.

The Hebrew teacher, Itzkhak "Cara" Schwartz, who has twelve students, walks to the kosher cantina after his class. He joins the young and old.

The gypsy Paul Babici, a master of klezmer music, prepares to play his saxophone. He is joined by his old friend, Itzkhak Gott, who has asked him to play. The horn and Itzkhak's accordion stir the air. And laughter and applause, by young and old, fill the cantina.

cluj

It is Shabbat and morning services have ended. Students file into the classroom, to be taught Hebrew by the melamed. Three young women, ages sixteen to eighteen, listen and respond. They are in the Beit Midrash adjacent to the Ohel Moshe Synagogue.

At about the time the lessons are ending, Rezele Abraham, ninety-three, sits down to eat her lunch at the kosher cantina. She enjoys the food and her friends, as she does every day.

There have been other days, when the girls were not at their Hebrew lessons, when Rezele has been joined by the three and by others like them. On those days they all joined in earnest and funny talk, enjoyed a kosher meal, paying little for the generously portioned lunch, nothing for the sharing of the tradition. Rezele and the girls know there will be other times; because that is what Cluj offers today, within the warmth of the kehilla.

Cluj (Kolozsvar in Hungarian, Klausen-burg in German) is in central Romania and is the cultural, industrial, and political center of Transylvania. Until 1920, and between 1940 and 1945, Transylvania was part of Hungary.

The first Jews of Cluj were Sephardics from Turkey, visiting the fairs of the sixteenth and seventeenth centuries. As was usual in Romania, during the eighteenth century the community became Ashkenazic. In 1807 the first prayer room was opened, and in 1818 the first synagogue was built. Life became unstable in the first half of the nineteenth century as laws barred Jews from certain jobs, from the right to buy and sell property, and from the right to have their own cemetery.

The national revolution in Hungary in 1848 led to the dual monarchy of Austria-Hungary, leading to legal Jewish residency and the flourishing of the kehilla.

Four disparate kehillot were established by the beginning of the twentieth century: the Neolog, Status Quo, Orthodox and Hasidic. Each maintained its own synagogues and schools, strongly guarding its religious and social philosophies. In 1920 Cluj became part of Romania. A distinction of the city's history was the establishment of a chapter of the World Zionist Organization in 1920. Cluj became and remained the center of the Zionist movement in Transylvania until the time of the Holocaust. The population grew to 15,000.

On August 30, 1940 Hungary was given northern Transylvania from Romania under the Vienna Award. Anti-Jewish measures and economic restrictions followed. In 1942, most able-bodied Jewish men were conscripted for forced labor on the Eastern Front.

In March 1944 the German occupation began. Nearly 70 percent of Cluj's kehillot perished in the city's ghetto and in Auschwitz. Only 6,500 returned after the war ended.

Three synagogues serve the remaining 500 Jews of the city. The Mare, known as the Deportatilor because from it Jews were deported to Auschwitz after being rounded up, was built by the Neolog kehilla in 1887, partially destroyed by German bombs in 1944, and restored with government funds in 1970. It gives minyan each Erev Shabbat and Shabbat, and on all holidays. The Ohel Moshe was established by the Orthodox kehilla and gives minyan twice each day. The beautifully ornate Status Quo synagogue Sas Khevra is used only during the summer, since it is too costly to heat during the other months.

The day is snowy, cold, and dirty at the old Jewish cemetery, which is connected to the Christian. The caretaker, a poorly-clad gentile, opens a gate to allow visitors in. They join wild goats and sheep that eat the hay put near the gravestones by the caretaker. The animals take no notice of the humans. The snow at the new cemetery is deep and unmarked by footprints.

Later in the day, an old, friendly man strikes up a conversation with a university student and a young musician as he sits in the Ohel Moshe shul. His Hebrew name is Avraham, and he invites the young men to his home for lunch. The musician's Hebrew name is Itzkhak, so Avraham tells him, "I'm your father since you are Itzkhak."

His home in the courtyard of the Sas Khevra shul is beautiful. He and his wife had been married to others before the Holocaust and had lost their spouses and their children. But they survived to find each other. Some Romanian kehillot may die soon. Because of Avraham and his wife, Rezele Abraham, and the university students who study, then stay, in Cluj, this city's kehilla may continue to live.

ROMAN

Gypsy musicians—a violinist, a drummer and two accordionists—play for Gilda and her attendants. Gilda is a bride, soon to be led to the khupa and her groom David.

David is from Dorohoi; she is from Roman.

The small city of Roman is in the Bacau province of northeast Moldavia. Its earliest Jews were traders who traveled from Turkey up the Danube to Siretul, establishing a small kehilla in the early sixteenth century. Its history was typical of most of Romania— the Jews expelled at the whim of a prince of Moldavia, the Jews persecuted at the behest of local priests.

As happened in Iasi, in 1893 Jewish pupils were barred from public schools, forcing the maintenance of modern Jewish elementary schools, and leading to a more potent kehilla. With the coming of legal status, of property ownership and rights to a cemetery, synagogues, and an educational system, the community grew to to 6,500, 40 percent of the city's population by the turn of the century.

Between 1900 and the Great War, Jews fled the chronic persecution, first for Western Europe, then the United States. By 1930, the population of the kehilla had dropped to 4,800.

The Holocaust brought deportation to Transnistria and the liquidation of many. But many escaped, many survived, and many came from outlying towns and villages, seeking better economic conditions. In 1947, Roman had 8,000 Jews.

The following years brought aliya to Israel. Today there are only 300 Jews left, with one operating synagogue, which gives daily minyan.

The gypsies have finished playing. Gilda is led under the khupa to join her groom David. Friends and family fall silent and listen. Rov Wasserman—who koshers chickens in Dorohoi on Wednesdays—begins a solemn droshe (speech) in Yiddish.

He speaks loudly and strongly. He invokes the history—the trials, the blood, the ashes, the Holocaust, and the destruction of the

Second Temple in Jerusalem. He speaks of murdered friends and family, and of the families that begin in weddings and save kehillot. With some of his words some of the women cry; with other words the crying rises to screams, as though the words were weights on the chests of the crying, as though those at the sacred wedding hear the cries of the dead living in the history. And he speaks of the wonder of being married Jewish, married in a Jewish wedding, stepping deeply into the tradition.

yugoslavia

ZAGREB

Inside the Jewish Home for the Aged it is as homey and warm as it is bitter and cold outside. Miriam has asked Olga, ninety-one, a question during their lunch. With a young voice, in unexpectedly clear English, Olga responds by teasing Miriam, now in her eighties, about her "youth." A young man approaches, pleased and shocked at the vibrancy and the English.

Olga smiles elegantly, explaining her English as a remnant of her six years in New York City from 1943 to 1949. Still startled by her apparent great health, the young man tells Olga she should live to 120. She responds: "Anything too much is not good. While I feel young: all right. When I feel old, then I'm ready to go."

In the thirteenth century Jews from France, Malta, and Albania settled in Zagreb. Chronicles from 1444 mention a "domus judaeorum" (community house or synagogue), and "magistratus judaeorum" (chief). During this period, Jews from Hungary and Moravia, mostly moneylenders and merchants, settled in Zagreb and all along the Sava, Drava, and Danube rivers.

The Austrians expelled the Jews in the sixteenth century and kept them out for 200 years. When Jews returned to the city, most were Ashkenazic, rather than Sephardic, as the original settlers had been.

In 1867 a beautiful synagogue was built in pseudo-Moorish style. It held the primary school, and the Talmud Torah reflected the prosperity the kehillot enjoyed. In 1873, the Jews received full civil liberties and the right to appeal to Budapest or Vienna for protection against anti-Semitic attacks.

In 1898 a union of high school students was formed, becoming the training ground for future Ha-Shomer Ha-Tzair and Zionist leaders. Consequently, between the world wars, the Zagreb kehillot became headquarters of the Yugoslavian Zionist Federation. This fervor was accompanied by organizations of Jewish women, Maccabi sports clubs, choirs, an orchestra, and Jewish journals and newspapers. The arts and literature, politics, and scholarship flourished, as did the sciences and commercial life. In 1931 the 12,000 Jews of Zagreb were well-to-do, the envy of those in the poorer provinces.

Then, in the mid-1930s, envy by neighbors—the German ethnic population—led to anti-Semitism, which became virulent as patriotic and nationalistic feelings were enflamed.

On April 10, 1941, Croatia declared independence, establishing a puppet government in Zagreb under Ante Pavelic, leader of the Ustachi, the fascist terrorists. Then came the taking of Jewish property, the registration of Jewish businesses, and the mandatory wearing of badges by all Jews. Mass arrests and shootings soon followed. Rabbi Marulies, the last rabbi of Zagreb, was shot. By October 1941, the majority of the city's Jews had been sent to forced labor camps. Survivors were shipped to Auschwitz in August 1942. When the persecution started there were 4,200 Jews in Zagreb. Forty percent returned after the war.

Flight to Israel has reduced the kehilla to 1,100. Today the synagogue is a single upstairs room in the kehilla office building. Kosher meat and Talmud Torah have disappeared. Friday night services draw twelve men, ten women. A Hebrew teacher from Belgrade teaches twenty, predominantly high school and college students, each Friday.

However, Dragan Volner, rosh kahal of the kehilla is encouraged. He maintains that *secular* Jewish life among students and young professionals is active and has been growing during this decade.

Symbolic of the complications of Jewish life is the 400-year-old Jewish cemetery. It is large and sits above the city, looking down at it. There are crypts of famous or wealthy Jews. Gravestones inscribed with names form part of the wall surrounding the cemetery. Some stones are elaborately carved. But the cemetery is shared. The Christians ran out of room in their cemetery and the Jews had to relinquish some of their burial space.

In the cemetery is a joint grave. There is a cross before a Jewish stone, representing a Catholic husband. He never converted, but wanted to be buried with his Jewish wife.

SARAJEVO

Thirty young children pretend to be bushes, small animals, and one small, old tree. It is the celebration of Tu B'Shevat in the clubhouse of the Ashkenazic synagogue. The tree symbolizes the Jews of Eastern Europe, the enduring group of communities that has survived exiles, expulsions, the Holocaust and the aftermath that has become the modern world.

Now it is time for the bag of goodies. Finished with their play, the children run to Rosita, the club coordinator, to get their simple, happy symbols of survival—prunes, peanuts, an apple, and a couple of sucking candies. Giggling, they sit down to devour the goodies. Rosita calls for music, and a violinist and a guitar-player stir the clubhouse with songs old and new, in Hebrew and Ladino.

This Jewish clubhouse, on other days, is a center for old and young. They watch television, play cards, read, play ping-pong and just sit and enjoy the company of each other. Sometimes the old ones will tell stories, in Ladino, of the partisans of World War II who refused to succumb to Nazis, women and

men who were then as young as the young ones who listen now. And the young ones often listen intently, against a background of portraits of young partisans who fought with Tito.

The first Jews of Sarajevo, Sephardic refugees from Spain, spoke Ladino. Their journey took them through Italy, Greece, and Bulgaria. They were artisans and merchants. Granted permission by their Turkish rulers, the Jews built a synagogue in 1581 and named it, in Spanish, Il Cal Grande. Destroyed by fire again and again, it has been rebuilt again and again.

Unlike their brethren in other Muslim countries, the Jews of the city could appear before Muslim religious courts in civil cases. Also, they were not forced to live in the Jewish quarter known as "El Cortijo." They established kehillot throughout the city and in other parts of Bosnia Hercegovina, of which Sarajevo was capital.

But a poll tax had to be paid and there were extortions and briberies. By the mid-seventeenth century, there was a Sephardic and an Askhenazic kehilla, the Ashkenazim having come from Central and Eastern Europe fleeing Christian persecution. The split remained until the Holocaust.

By the mid-nineteenth century, all of Sarajevo's doctors were Jews. Other Jews were artisans and merchants, blacksmiths, tailors, shoemakers, joiners, metal workers, butchers, and traders in iron, wood, textiles, furs, and glass. Jews operated the first sawmill. With all this vitality, the kehillot reached 2,100 persons in 1850.

In 1878, Austria-Hungary annexed Bosnia, sending Ashkenazim from Austria, Hungary, Galicia, and Poland to the city. Entrepreneurs and intellectuals, they brought wealth and power.

The creation of the Kingdom of Yugoslavia in 1918 was a boon to the Jews. Social and benevolent organizations thrived, among them La Benevolencia and Lyra, a choir that promoted Ladino folk music.

In 1928 a theological seminary was opened, offering secondary education as well as rabbinical studies. It was the only rabbinical seminary in the Balkans. Today Rabbi Zadeek Danon is the only rabbi in Yugoslavia, and he is a graduate of this school. In 1931, the palatial synagogue of the Ashkenazim was completed.

Between the two world wars, Sarajevo was the third largest kehilla in Yugoslavia (after Zagreb and Belgrade). It contained 8,318 persons in 1935.

On March 25, 1941 there were 13,000 Jews in Sarajevo, nearly 80 percent of them Sephardim. Then Yugoslavia joined the Axis. The indiscriminate killing and destruction began at once.

Mass deportations began in October 1941—children and the elderly sent directly to the Jasenovac death camp. The able-bodied were forced to labor in the camp of Djakova and the island of Rab. Andrija Artukovic, Minister of Interior and Police in the puppet government of Croatia, led the ruthless Ustachi troops that ran these camps.

Meanwhile 973 Jews of Sarajevo battled the Nazis, side-by-side with the communist partisans. Three hundred forty were killed. By the end of the war, few Jews survived.

The kehilla struggled to recover, but between 1948 and 1949 most survivors chose aliya to Israel.

Now the Ashkenazic synagogue is the focal point of the community. But there is no kosher kitchen. The kosher foods available— wine, salami, chickens, gefilte fish—are imported from Israel. The matzoh for Passover is from Holland. Ten to twelve Jews study Hebrew once each week. The holidays and festivals—such as that of Tu B'Shevat— take place in the community center, the clubhouse.

Three kilometers from the clubhouse, the cemetery lies beyond an old cobblestone road. It was carved out of a steep hill and terraced. The gravestones are in a very ancient Roman style and startle with their severity. Visitors must climb through theick, hazardous, thorny brush to get to the stones.

The Vacra memorial was built by the

government in 1982. It remembers the 10,000 victims of a pogrom in the streets of the city. The 10,000 names line the interior of the memorial—7,500 Jewish names, the rest the names of Christians and Muslims. All were murdered by Croatian and German fascists.

ΠΟVΙ-SΔΟ

It is a day of snow and a day of a concert, of classical music, for the citizens of the city. Concert-goers file through the door of the synagogue. They are not Jews. Religious services are held only during the High Holidays; the kehilla leases the synagogue the rest of the year. Some concert-goers stop on the walk before the building and admire the architecture. They are the ones who pause to see the Hebrew inscription above the door, which reads:

"Because my house is the house of prayer it is open to all nations."

On the High Holidays, the Jews reclaim their prayer house and walk under the inscription. But, lacking a religious leader to lead the prayers, they listen to recordings. On records, they hear the Rosh Hashana and Yom Kippur liturgy sung by the famous cantors Jan Peerce, Moshe Koussevitzky, and Yossele Rosenblatt. Most celebrants sing along with the record.

Sephardim began to arrive in Novi-Sad in the sixteenth and seventeenth centuries, under Ottoman rule. They thrived as merchants, physicians, and artisans. They were allowed to own land. Austria took the city from the Turks in 1699, however, and the Jews suffered plundering and murder. Survivors were sold as slaves in Austria or forced to flee to Bulgaria. By the beginning of the eighteenth century, Ashkenazim from Moravia had replaced the Sephardic kehilla, which had vanished.

When Joseph II ruled, there was forced assimilation and Jews had to learn German or Hungarian in order to open a business or marry. They also were forced to have formal education, increasing the power over them of the secular state. In 1802 a Jewish school was built. In 1820 a hospital rose. During the Hungarian revolution of 1848 both were destroyed.

Novi-Sad (Ujvidek in Hungarian) is in the Vojvodina province, which became part of the Yugoslav Kingdom in 1918. The Jews of the city already had been imbued with the Hungarian culture and were Magyars of the Jewish faith. Serbian Jews, to the south, on the other hand, became a recognized minority after the Great War. They were strong supporters of Zionism.

During the 1920s and 1930s the kehilla prospered and grew to 4,400 souls.

April 1941 saw the annexation of Novi-Sad by Hungary. Occupation by the Hungarians and Germans continued until September 1944. Extermination came in waves. On January 21-23, 1942 a horrible "aktion" took place, using as an excuse a small labor camp rebellion near the city. Jewish homes were searched and plundered, the Jews inside murdered. Fifteen hundred Jews and 500 Serbs were marched to the Danube, lined up, shot in the back, and thrown in the river. Then the Iron Guard of Budapest ordered an end to the massacres and a gathering of all Jewish men between eighteen and forty-five. They were put in labor battalions in Hungary and the Ukraine. Most died from maltreatment and starvation. Tito's partisans and Soviet troops liberated the city on October 20, 1944.

Only 900 Jews returned after the war.

The last rabbi of Novi-Sad died in 1948, but the city maintained a daily minyan for the next thirty years. It took place in the beautiful synagogue—built in 1906 (the third on the site, the first built in 1717)—now leased to the city. Through those years, many of the kehilla left for Israel. Now there are 300, half of whom are active.

It is night at the Jewish club and for the fifty here, including young teenagers, there are platters of oranges, raisins, peanuts, and dried figs. There is laughter, singing, and the sound of a violin. Also, there is talk, some retelling of history by the old to the young. One of the men in the room is named Sosberger. He has been a rosh kahal and is the local historian. His family has lived in the city 200 years, tracing their roots to Czechoslovakia. He is a retired architect who now writes and speaks of the tradition. One of two boys, he survived the "aktion" of January 21-23, 1942. His brother was killed.

His children live in the city and have married Jewish spouses.

Among those raptly listening is a young soldier named Zoran. His grandmother was Jewish, but was forced to convert by the Nazi terror. She reconverted after the Holocaust. His mother married a non-Jew and became a strong member of the Communist Party. But Zoran remembers his Jewishness. Quietly and fervently he tells of his plan to be circumcised.

BELGRADE

Rabbi Zadeek Danon begins the Friday night prayer. He returns to his tuning pipe again and again, seeking to find just the right key for the prayer. He wears special Shabbat clothes, resembling those worn by Reform rabbis in the United States.

Late in the thirteenth century, Jews from Italy and Hungary settled permanently in Belgrade (Beograd in Serbian).

The Turks conquered the city in 1521. Sephardic Jews arrived soon after, and formed a kehilla under the Ottoman rule. By 1663, the community numbered 800 and had the right to its own land. They were physicians, merchants, weaponsmiths, and tanners. And they were relatively prosperous. With the seventeenth century, German and Hungarian refugees came and built a yeshiva that became widely known.

Catastrophe came to the Jews in the late seventeenth century. The Turks were forced to defend the city against the Austrians, and they vented their anger on the Jews, plundering and burning the Jewish quarter.

The Austrians took the city. They burned, looted and killed both Turks and Jews. Surviving Jews were taken to Austria to be sold as slaves or were offered to kehillot for ransom. The city kept changing hands, each time trapping the Jews in the middle of the fight. But the Jews maintained themselves through the unstable years, and by 1831 numbered 1,300. Eleven hundred were Sephardim, the rest Ashkenazim.

An age of assimilation began in 1878, with Jewish legal rights granted by the Congress of Berlin. Wealthy Jews adopted Serbian culture, speaking Serbian in their homes and sending their children to state schools and universities to become civil servants, physicians, and lawyers.

The Sephardic kehilla built the Beit Yisrael Synagogue in 1907. By 1931 it was composed of 45 percent of the Jews of Belgrade, second-largest in Europe, behind Salonika, Greece. Jewish poets, writers, and composers wrote in Ladino, describing Sephardic life and using both Jewish and non-Jewish themes.

Most of these artists were murdered in the Holocaust.

The Germans occupied Belgrade in April 1941, finding 12,000 Jews living there. Within a week, Jews were forced to register and wear the Star of David badge. Twenty thousand Volkdeutsche (ethnic Germans) eagerly assisted the occupiers in identifying Jews and Jewish businesses, and themselves plundered as they could. The Ashkenazic synagogue—used today—was made a brothel. In May 1941 all men fourteen to sixty and all women fourteen to forty were forced into labor brigades.

Jewish armed resistance began at once, and was symbolized by the Jewish youth of the Ha-Shomer Ha-Tzaiv. They became conspicuous to their comrades for bravery and determination in sabotaging enemy installations and collecting money and medical supplies.

Their bravery brought the usual response: "aktions" which killed several hundred Jews.

The "final solution" came to the Jews of Belgrade before the death camps were fully operational. Therefore, 5,000 Jews were told they were being taken to Austria for work. They were shot en masse in the forests outside Belgrade between October and December 1941. The remaining 6,000 died of starvation, disease, freezing weather, or the infamous gas vans.

The liberation by the Russians in October 1944 brought the return of only 200 Jews to the city. The Sephardic and Ashkenazic kehillot then joined into one community. It used the Ashkenazic synagogue, freeing it from its life as a brothel under the Nazis.

In 1947, the kehilla numbered 2,271, half of whom emigrated to Israel as soon as it became a state. The kehilla now is the largest in Yugoslavia: 1,600. Three teachers teach twenty-two students Hebrew.

For five days the National Conference on Yugoslavian Jewry goes on. Rabbi Danon weaves Ladino folk songs through the speeches by musicians, writers, composers, politicians, and historians. They all have two things in common: they have survived the Holocaust and they have been partisans under Marshal Tito. Tito's portrait looks down from the wall at the survivors.

It is Saturday night at the conference, the time of food, drink, and song. Eugene "Moshe" Weber performs Yiddish folksongs with pent-up enthuasism. He is joined by a man on a guitar, and they play Hebrew, Yiddish, and Israeli folk music until midnight.

BULGARIA

SOfIA

The Bulgarian government is restoring the interior of the magnificent Beit Knesset Sofia Synagogue. Here, above the Holy Ark, is written: "Know before whom you stand."

It is Friday night and the Sephardic community's khazan Chaim Meshulam leads services. Two young men approach and assist the religious leader. The two have studied at the Rabbinical Seminary in Budapest. This Friday as always the young help the old go on.

Jews came to Bulgaria in the first century, under the Romans. When the Empire was split in 293, the territories of the east Mediterranean became known as the Byzantine Empire, and the Jews of Sofia belonged to the sect called Romaniots. They spoke Greek, had their own prayer books and customs, and were the majority of the kehilla until the fifteenth century.

Expulsion of Jews from Hungary in 1376, and from Bavaria in 1470, formed the core of the first Ashkenazic kehilla in Sofia. Jews expelled from Spain and Portugal in 1492 and 1496, respectively, formed the core of the Sephardic kehilla. Until 1640, therefore, there were three kehillot: the Romaniot, the Ashkenazic, and the Sephardic.

Up to the mid-nineteenth century the Jews worked as artisans and businessmen. They enjoyed the economic power that came from Sofia's being the transit center for commerce from Thessalonika to Belgrade and Bucharest. The kehilla grew to 3,000.

Bulgaria became independent in 1878, having defeated Turkey. The 4,146 Jews of Sofia were praised highly by the general community for their defense of the city, particularly for the way they guarded it against fire. However, the praise soon turned to Jew-baiting influenced by the rabid anti-Semitism coming from Russia. Several thousand Jews fled to the United States and Anatolia (in Asia Minor).

By 1940, the kehilla had grown to 29,000. By this time daily life had come to mean fear and caution, as the Bulgarian government had turned more and more pro-German. Anti-Jewish laws came in July 1941 including a special tax on Jewish property, a curfew, and the confiscation of personal and business telephones and radios.

A special commission to handle the "Jewish problem" was created. Its goal was deportation of all of the city's Jews, first to rural towns far from the eyes of the general public, then to the death camps. But the project of extermination was not carried out.

The kehilla had Zionist roots older than the Holocaust. In the years after the war, 20,000 Jews journeyed to Israel. Today there are few Jews in Bulgaria, most of them in the kehilla in Sofia.

Important to the kehilla in Sofia is the Jewish club. Each day, from three to seven in the afternoon, there is food, backgammon, chess, and the time of sharing each other's company. The air is bright and lively.

It is a Friday afternoon at the club. Itzkhak Levi, as he often does, is playing chess against two young men at the same time. After winning, as he often does, he invites his challengers to his home, near the club, for the Friday night meal. His apartment is warm but without Jewish objects. But Itzkhak speaks with his daughter and son-in-law in Hebrew. The talk is of Israel and of the tradition. Shabbat candles are lit. The foods are ethnic.

It is Shabbat morning in the synagogue. The only woman in attendance takes the Torah cover and folds it. After the reading, when the Torah is prepared to be returned to the Ark, she extends the mantle to the khazzan. She moves with the ease of one who often does this. A few moments pass and the shamash serves kiddush—sugar cookies and strong Turkish coffee.

plovdiv

Plovdiv has tree-lined boulevards. It also has cobblestone streets. One of them, particularly old, particularly cracked, passes through the Jewish courtyard, past the Beit Midrash (small Orthodox synagogue). On this Wednesday afternoon only two persons pass—one young girl, one old man.

In the courtyard of the abandoned Beit Knesset Zion, where he lives, the shamash, David Kahan remembers when the kehilla was not so quiet, when the synagogue was filled with the sounds of prayers and the life of the community.

But now the only use for the lovely building is restricted to its back door, where death notices are posted to announce the passing of a member of the kehilla.

A treasure has been unearthed in Plovdiv—parts of a mosaic floor and panels depicting a menorah. They were parts of a synagogue that stood in 290, created by Jewish tradesmen and craftsmen. They had come from Palestine and Syria searching for trade routes along the Maritsa River that passed Thrace on its way into the Aegean Sea.

Plovdiv suffered many sacks during the Middle Ages, and the Jews suffered harassment as they were blamed for the city's woes and persecuted. Turkish control, beginning in 1364, meant centuries of relative peace for the kehilla. The city prospered as an agricultural region centered on the Belgrade-Sofia-Istanbul trade route, and the kehilla prospered also.

In 1786 Rabbi Abraham ibn Aroiio (1750-1819) led the building of the first synagogue since that small, ancient one.

After the Russo-Turkish War of 1877-78, Plovdiv became capital of the Turkish vassal state of Eastern Rumelia. Jews were a major part of the vassal assembly, voting predominantly for the Bulgarian Party, which led to the annexation of Eastern Rumelia by Bulgaria in 1885.

With the coming of the twentieth century, the kehilla became consumed with Zionism. In 1924 the national Zionist headquarters was placed here. Commerce in textiles and furniture and leathercraft were the economic mainstay of the kehilla, which reached its peak in 1940, with 7,000 persons.

With the dawn of 1941 came anti-Jewish laws, including the mandatory wearing of the Star of David badge. SS Attaché Theodor Dannecker began the deportation. The unemployed, sick, and elderly were sent to Sofia buildings marked with the Star of David. But the Jews of Plovdiv went no farther. They survived.

Emigration to Israel reduced the kehilla's members sharply: 5,800 in 1946; 1,000 in 1967; 500 today.

On this bright, chilly Wednesday, a man waves to a friend in the street. He is standing on the terrace of his apartment, which is part of a complex that houses 60 percent of the kehilla population. The complex stands where Beit Yeshurun Synagogue, the one built in 1786 by Rabbi Abraham, had stood for two centuries The State tore it down in 1965, when the failing kehilla no longer could afford to keep up the synagogue.

In the desolate, unused Beit Knesset Zion Synagogue of Shamash David, a plaque hangs, which was donated in 1922 by the Benevolent Society for Orphans. It reads: "These are the names of our heroic brothers who spilled their blood to protect our country Bulgaria, and honored our people in the Balkan and World War."

It is Friday afternoon and it is raining in

the Plovdiv cemetery. The stones are broken, fallen, and overturned. At their insistence, the elderly rosh kahal Avram Behar has brought two young visitors here. Embarrassed at the ruins, he says, in simple Hebrew: "Ha-ir ha-ya gadol a-vol, ketsat yeladim ain beit sefer shoom davar" [The city was big but few children, no school—nothing].

No one else is in the cemetery.

Facing: Zipporah Greenglass, a resident of the Jewish Home for the Aged. *Dorohoi, Romania.*
Above: Naphtali Blau, the shamash in the shul on Heydukova Street. *Bratislava, Czechoslovakia.*

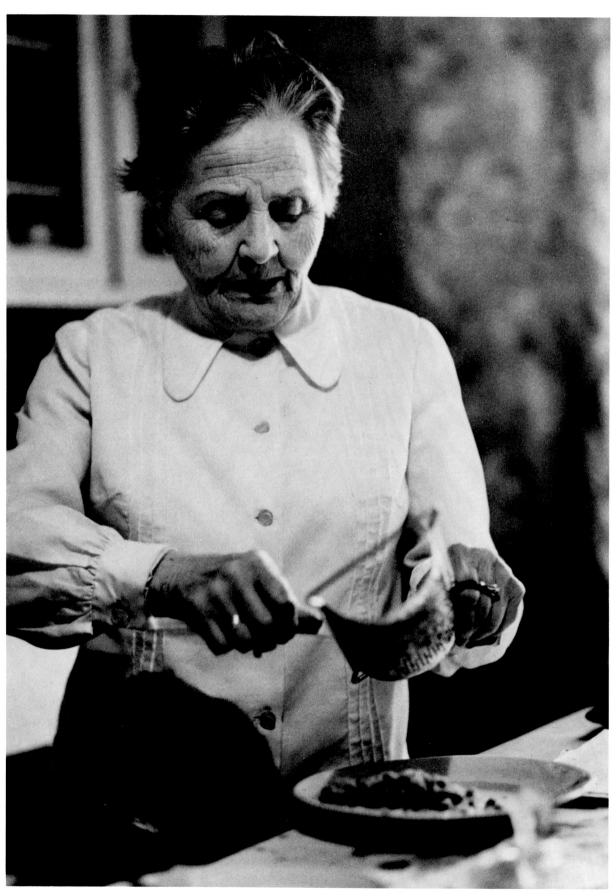

Above: Chana Najbaum, a staunch Communist. *Walbrzych, Poland.*
Facing: Mrs. Waltraut Stecher and her son Denny. *Prague, Czechoslovakia.*

Four rabbis of the Rabbinical Seminary share food and wine.
Budapest, Hungary.

Facing: Ludovit Arye Dojc, leader of the Yiddish club and an historian of Jewish Czechoslovakian cemeteries. *Bratislava, Czechoslovakia*.

Below: Miriam and Olga enjoying an afternoon snack in the Jewish Home for the Aged. *Zagreb, Yugoslavia*.

Above: Rezele Abraham, ninety-three, at the kosher cantina. *Cluj, Romania.*
Facing: Mrs. Cohen sitting alone in the Jewish Home for
the Aged. *Zagreb, Yugoslavia.*

Above: Dr. Edith Varga, with patients and staff of the
Calea Calarasi Jewish Old Age Home. *Bucharest, Romania.*
Facing: David Kahan, shamash of the abandoned Beit
Knesset Zion. *Plovdiv, Romania.*

Above: After Shabbat services, friends gather in the Martirok synagogue. *Nyiregyhaza, Hungary.*
Facing: A man reading the Yiddish weekly newspaper,
Folkstimme, in the lounge of the kehilla's large central
building. *Krakow, Poland.*

Above: Reading and conversation in the Jewish club.
Sarajevo, Yugoslavia.
Facing: Moshe Joseph Goldman sits under a poster adver-
tising a production of the Yiddish theater. *Dzierzoniow,
Poland.*

Facing : Woman leaving the Great Shul. *Sofia, Bulgaria.*
Below: Woman in the Jewish Home for the Aged. *Dorohoi,*
Romania.

KÓSER HÙSBOLT
ITT

Facing: An old woman walks past the courtyard door of
synagogue Beit Knesset. *Sofia, Bulgaria.*
Above: Sweeping the entrance to the courtyard in front
of the kosher butcher shop. *Miskolc, Hungary.*

Above: Man leaving the Jewish cultural house. *Wroclaw, Poland.*
Facing, top: Intersection of Sholem Aleichem and Bogdan Chmielnicki Streets.
Odessa, U.S.S.R.
Facing, bottom: At the end of Josefovska Street, in the heart of the old Jewish
quarter, the Pinkas synagogue. Its foundations date from the tenth century.
Prague, Czechoslovakia

Facing, top: Former Hebrew gymnasium shut down in 1968. *Dzierzoniow, Poland.*
Facing, bottom: A farmer passing the Rindalior synagogue built by Jewish farmers a hundred years ago. The building is destined to be razed, to make way for an apartment complex. *Dorohoi, Romania.*
Top: Woman hauling cart, passing the synagogue and kosher butcher shop. *Nyiregyhaza, Hungary.*
Above: Horse-drawn sleigh. *Dorhoi, Romania.*

Facing: A typical quiet weekday in the Jewish courtyard. *Novi-Sad, Yugoslavia*.
Below: Mausoleum in the Jewish cemetery. *Zagreb, Yugoslavia*.
Bottom: A small street on which the Jewish club is located. *Dzierzoniow, Poland*.

Facing: Yakimovsky Pereulok Street; Beit Knesset
Kishinev at the far end of the street. *Kishinev, U.S.S.R.*
Below: A mikvah, now largely unused. *Nyiregyhaza, Hungary.*

Above: Yankel Deutsch, seventy-eight years old, a kosher
butcher. *Miskolc, Hungary.*
Facing: Sign outside the kosher butcher shop. *Budapest,
Hungary.*

ORTH. KÓSER
SZALÁMI ÉS
KOLBÁSZÁRU ÜZEM
← KAZINCZY U. 41. SZ.
AZ UDVARBAN

Facing: Itzkhak, seventy-nine years old (left), and Morde-
cai Goldburger, eighty-one years old, who work in the
kosher kitchen located in the courtyard of the shul.
Kosice, Czechoslovakia.
Above: Cooks in the kosher kitchen, in a part of the
former Breslau Seminary. Only Esther (left) is Jewish.
Wroclaw, Poland.

Above: Miriam Weiss with a chicken she will prepare for
her husband, the shokhet. *Budapest, Hungary.*
Facing: Shokhet Itzkhak Weiss at work. He is the only
shokhet for the city. *Budapest, Hungary.*

Right: Courtyard of the shul. *Odessa, U.S.S.R.*
Below: Matzoh factory. *Odessa, U.S.S.R.*
Facing: The challah baker. *Budapest, Hungary.*

Facing: Woman working in the kosher bakery. *Budapest, Hungary.*
Below: Exterior of the only Jewish-owned store in the city. *Miskolc, Hungary.*

David Lanceberg in his clothing shop, the only privately owned Jewish business in the city. He survived the war in Tashkent, Uzbekistan. *Wroclaw, Poland.*

Facing: Hannah-Rivkah Landsman in her hat shop. *Budapest, Hungary.*

Top: Andras Lautman at the counter of his watch shop. *Miskolc, Hungary.*

Above: János Hohlfeld, a metalworker. He is allowed to make and sell Jewish metalwork provided he also sells Christian objects. *Budapest, Hungary.*

Listening to Rov Wasserman reading the Megillah Esther on the morning of an ufruf during Purim in the Beit Midrash of Beit Solomon. *Dorohoi, Romania.*

Right: Shamash Benjamin in the
courtyard of the shul. *Kosice,
Czechoslovakia.*
Below: Caroline and Jozsef Samuel.
Vac, Hungary.
Facing: The shokhet's wife (left)
talks with a friend bringing chickens
to be koshered. *Miskolc, Hungary.*

A lecture in the Jewish museum during the National Conference on Yugoslavian Jewry. On the wall is a portrait of Marshal Tito. *Belgrade, Yugoslavia.*

Facing, top: Hasid Rabbi Itzkhak Goldberg (left), born in Budapest and visiting from New York, involved in a discussion of the Talmud at the Kazinczy synagogue. *Budapest, Hungary.*

Facing, bottom: Moshe Schwartz discusses kehilla business with a neighbor. *Warsaw, Poland.*

Below: Two members of the kehilla meet in the kosher kitchen. *Warsaw, Poland.*

Below: Kiddush after morning services. *Kishinev, U.S.S.R.*
Facing, top: A backgammon game at a Jewish club. *Sofia, Bulgaria.*
Facing, bottom: The author playing violin in the kosher kitchen. *Debrecen, Hungary.*

Above: Young Jewish soldier visits the Jewish club. *Novi-Sad, Yugoslavia*.
Facing: An old man at morning services proudly wearing his medal of valor from World War II. *Odessa, U.S.S.R.*

Facing: A peasant woman delivering kosher fowl for the shokhet. *Dorohoi, Romania.*
Below: Outside synagogue Beit Solomon, two women wait for Rov Wasserman, the shokhet, who koshers meat every Wednesday. *Dorohoi, Romania.*

Above: A glass of schnapps after morning services at the Kazinczy shul. *Budapest, Hungary.*
Right: Horse-drawn delivery wagon. *Dzierzoniow, Poland.*

The last building of the old Jewish ghetto. "Ulica Zidovska" means "Jewish Street." *Bratislava, Czechoslovakia.*

Facing: Rabbi Marulies walks from the Mare synagogue
to his home in its courtyard. *Bucharest, Romania.*
Above: Rabbi Yidl Weiss, a Satmar hasid, serves the
kehilla as shokhet. *Miskolc, Hungary.*

Below: An old woman arranges with the shamash to recite the kaddish for her husband's yartzeit. *Odessa, U.S.S.R.*
Facing: In the Ohel Moshe shul. *Cluj, Romania.*

Below: An old man stands by the stove in the Tailors' Wives' shul. *Bucharest, Romania.*
Facing: Abraham the shamash with candlesticks to be cleaned. *Dorohoi, Romania.*

Studying with Rabbi Yidl Weiss in the Beit Midrash.
Miskolc, Hungary.

Facing: The late Rabbi Dr. Alexander Scheiber, former leader of the Rabbinical Seminary, cuts the challah. *Budapest, Hungary*.

Above: Bela Hap waiting for the English mohel to touch his lips with the wine of the Covenant. Known in the kehilla as Ephraim, he is completing his brit at the age of forty-one. At the left is the local mohel, Yaakov Herzog, at the right the London physician who performed the circumcision. *Budapest, Hungary*.

Facing: Josef Schlaf with one of the books in his remark-
able collection of Hebrew and Yiddish works. *Warsaw,
Poland*.
Above: Moshe Jakubowicz, leader of the Jewish community, with photographs of the thirty-fifth anniversary
celebration of the kehilla. *Dzierzoniow, Poland*.

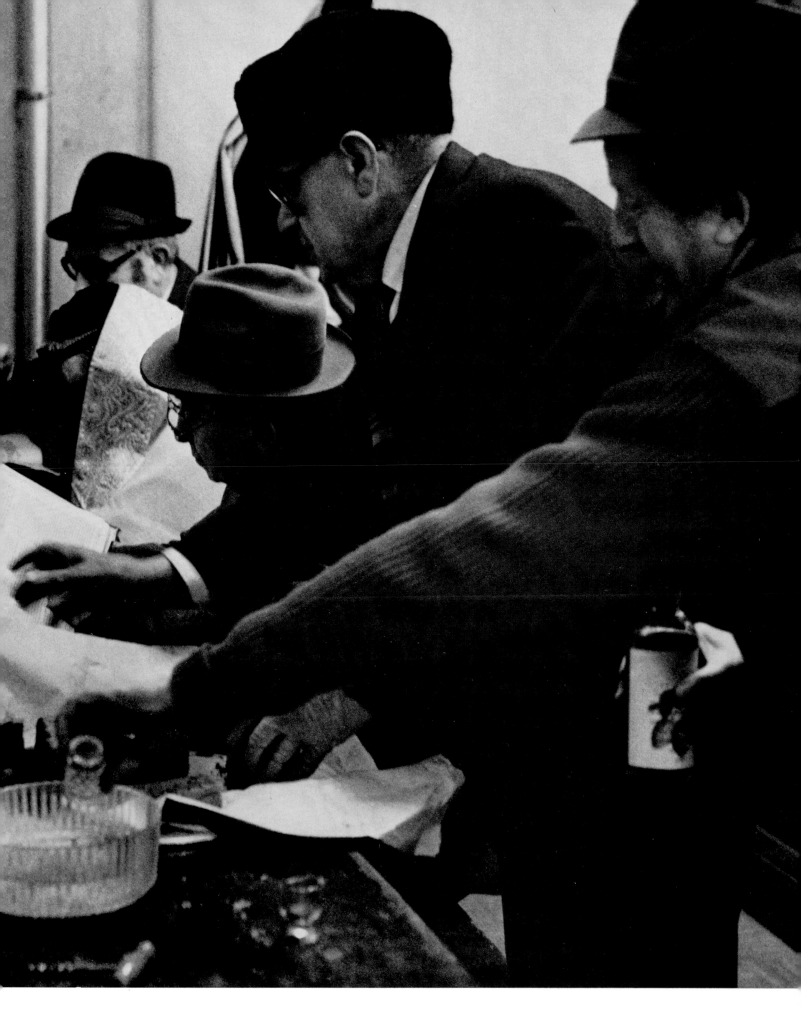

The Talmud is studied, and wine is served for kiddush at
the Orthodox shul. *Budapest, Hungary.*

The Jewish club during Tu B'Shevat celebration. *Novi-Sad, Yugoslavia.*

Below: The shamash collects tzedakah at the Bikur Cho-
lim synagogue, known as the Desseffwy Shul for the
street on which it stands. *Budapest, Hungary*.
Facing: Students and teachers gather for services in the
Leo Frankel synagogue. *Budapest, Hungary*.

Cantor Chaim Meshulam recites Friday night kiddush. *Sofia, Bulgaria.*

Above: Prayer books in the window of the Desseffwy
Shul. *Budapest, Hungary.*
Facing, top: Men daven at the Desseffwy Shul. *Budapest,
Hungary.*
Facing, bottom: Old books—some dating from the eight-
eenth century—in a room in a synagogue courtyard.
Kosice, Czechoslovakia.

Facing: Plaque containing the words of the blessing to be given before the Torah is read. They are transliterated from Hebrew into Bulgarian for those who cannot read Hebrew. *Sofia, Bulgaria.*
Above: Rabbi Zadeek Danon, the only rabbi in the country, makes kiddush. *Belgrade, Yugoslavia.*

Above: Rabbi Dauber leading morning prayers. *Iasi, Romania*.

Facing: Morning services at Beit Knesset, built in 1884. *Kishinev, U.S.S.R.*

Clockwise, from left: Poale Zion synagogue, leased by the city from the kehilla, now used as a theater warehouse on the south bank of the Somescu-Mic River. *Cluj, Romania*. Gypsies clearing the snow before the Tailors' Synagogue, now a museum. *Bucharest, Romania*. The Alte-Neue Shul, established in the mid-thirteenth century. The lower clock on the Jewish communal building built at the end of the sixteenth century, in the background, gives the hours in Hebrew. *Prague, Czechoslovakia*. The Mare synagogue, known among the local Jews as the Deportatilor synagogue, used by the Nazis to gather Jews destined for Auschwitz during World War II. *Cluj, Romania*. Obituary notices on the back door of a closed synagogue. *Plovdiv, Bulgaria*. Central Shul, used as a stable by the Nazis. After the war it was used as a garage, a matzoh factory, and currently a warehouse for the kehilla. *Cluj, Romania*.

Clockwise, from left: Beit Knesset Sofia, the largest Sephardic synagogue in Europe, built in 1909. The only synagogue in the city, it is being refurbished with government funds. *Sofia, Bulgaria*. The Choral Temple, where Chief Rabbi Dr. Moses Rosen has his pulpit. *Bucharest, Romania*. Entrance to Beit Knesset Puskinova, no longer in use; it is leased to the city as a book repository. *Kosice, Czechoslovakia*. The only synagogue that survived World War II is leased to the city for concerts, but holds services on the High Holidays. *Novi-Sad, Yugoslavia*. The Ashkenazic synagogue, the only one remaining in the city. During World War II it was used as a Nazi brothel. *Belgrade, Yugoslavia*. Sas Khevra synagogue, used only in warm weather as heating is too costly. *Cluj, Romaina*.

Upper left: Beit Knesset Kishinev, the only one left of the fifty-six synagogues in Kishinev. *Kishinev, U.S.S.R.*

Upper center: Beit Knesset Roman, built in 1900. *Roman, Romania.*

Upper right: The Mare synagogue, built in the seventeenth century. Hasidic leader Rabbi Abraham Joshua Heschel ("Apter Rov") worshipped here in 1820. *Iasi, Romania.*

Center, left: Abandoned yeshiva. *Krakow, Poland.*

Center, middle: Beit Knesset Zion, built in 1895, now closed. *Plovdiv, Bulgaria.*

Center, right: The Ashkenazic synagogue, focal point of the Jewish community today. *Sarajevo, Yugoslavia.*

Lower left: The Alte Shul, Poland's oldest existing synagogue, dates from the time of King Casimir the Great in the fourteenth century. Now a museum of Polish Jewish culture, it is one of only three synagogues declared national monuments by the Polish government. *Krakow, Poland.*

Left: The Dohanyi synagogue, which can hold over 3,000 worshippers, is the largest active synagogue in Europe today. Built in 1859, it was used during World War II to gather Jews being sent to Auschwitz. *Budapest, Hungary.*

Right: Small Status Quo shul. *Debrecen, Hungary.*

Center, left: Shul built in 1857, now being restored with government financial support. *Dzierzoniow, Poland.*

Below: A Talmud Torah in the Jewish quarter Kazimierz, before the Holocaust, now the site of an apartment building. *Krakow, Poland.*

Lower left: The Great Synagogue, built in 1861. *Miskolc, Hungary.*

Lower right: A Moorish style Jerusalem shul. The inscription above its entrance, from the Psalms, reads: This is the Lord's gate through which the righteous shall enter. *Prague, Czechoslovakia.*

Below, left: Exterior of the abandoned Status Quo synagogue. Above the entrance to the synagogue the inscription reads: My dwelling you will see. *Vac, Hungary.*
Below, right: Interior of the abandoned Status Quo synagogue. *Vac, Hungary.*
Facing: Orthodox synagogue, active daily. *Debrecen, Hungary.*

Clockwise, from upper left: Interior of the Mare synagogue. Note the inscriptions on the lights, each donated by a family in memory of someone who has passed away. *Dorohoi, Romania*. Interior of the synagogue. *Novi-Sad, Yugoslavia*. Interior of the Ashkenazic synagogue. *Sarajevo, Yugoslavia*. Inside the Great Synagogue. *Miskolc, Hungary*. Interior of the recently renovated Nozick Shul, the only synagogue in Warsaw today. *Warsaw, Poland*. Inside unused Beit Knesset Zion. *Plovdiv, Bulgaria*.

Facing, above: Shamash Benjamin with the cemetery care-taker, a gentile. She carries the casket cover of a man just buried. *Kosice, Czechoslovakia.*

Facing, below: Goodbye to a friend and kehilla member. *Kosice, Czechoslovakia.*

Top: A funeral. *Bratislava, Czechoslovakia.*

Above: A burial in the kehilla's 200-year-old cemetery. *Warsaw, Poland.*

Above: Ruined Jewish cemetery. *Plovdiv, Bulgaria.*
Right: Vandalized cemetery, *Kishinev, U.S.S.R.*
Below: Old cemetery begun in 1759. *Miskolc, Hungary.*

Left: Old Jewish cemetery. *Dorohoi, Romania*.
Below: Goats graze in a nineteenth century Orthodox cemetery. *Cluj, Romania*.

Right: Here lie the remains of the 12,000 Jewish victims murdered by Romanian and German soldiers on June 28-29, 1941. *Iasi, Romania*.
Below: The oldest existing Jewish cemetery in Poland, begun in 1564. *Krakow, Poland*.
Below, right: A room once used for ritual purification and preparation for burial in an old Jewish cemetery, now closed. *Novi-Sad, Yugoslavia*.

Clockwise, from facing top: Interior of Vacra memorial to Jews, Moslems, and Christians killed by German and Croatian fascists during World War II. *Sarajevo, Yugoslavia.*

Holocaust memorial which reads: These we will remember for it is poured in my soul. Here was buried soap made from our brothers, people of Israel, who were killed in the name of God by the Nazis of Germany in 1944. May God erase their names. Several of them were buried here at the end of the war 1945. *Nyiregyhaza, Hungary.*

Monument to the Jews, Moslems, and Serbs murdered during the infamous "aktion" of January 21-23, 1942, in which 7,500 Jews were killed. *Novi-Sad, Yugoslavia.*

Lighting candles at the wall of the old cemetery in the courtyard of the Dohanyi Synagogue, on the fortieth anniversary of the city's liberation during World War II. *Budapest, Hungary.*

War memorial plaque remembering Jewish soldiers in a closed synagogue. It states: These are the names of our heroic brothers who spilled their blood to protect our country, Bulgaria, and honored our people in the Balkan and World War. *Plovdiv, Bulgaria.*

In the old cemetery on the fortieth anniversary of the city's liberation during World War II. *Budapest, Hungary.*

Above: Caretaker (center) of the Jewish cemetery with his wife and his son. *Cluj, Romania.*

Facing: Stone piano in a huge Ashkenazic cemetery in memory of a promising young composer who perished of typhus fever contracted in a work camp in Transnistria. *Bucharest, Romania.*

Above, left: An overturned gravestone in the Jewish cemetery. *Sofia, Bulgaria*.

Above, right: In the 300-year-old Sephardic cemetery, a young boy's picture hangs on his newly placed gravestone. On the tree are notices of his and other recent deaths. *Sofia, Bulgaria*.

Above: Gravestones in the Sephardic cemetery, cut in the ancient Roman style. *Sarajevo, Yugoslavia*.

Top: The gravestone of Chaia Liwschitz. Her epitaph reads: Freedom fighter lost her life along with millions of her comrades fighting for freedom. *Cluj, Romania*.

Above: The Kafka family monument in the Jewish cemetry. *Prague, Czechoslovakia*.

Left: Grave of the Kallo Rebbe, Itzkhak of Taub, who brought Hasidism to Hungary. Satmar Hasidim from the United States, Europe, and Israel visit this gravesite annually on the yartzeit, the 7th of Adar. *Nagykallo, Hungary*.

The shamash, Yankel Weiss, collects money after a funeral, according to custom. He will give it to the woman who brought a bucket of water and a towel for washing the hands of those leaving the cemetery. *Debrecen, Hungary.*

Below: The abandoned Breslau Jewish Theological Seminary, established by Rabbi Zachariah Frankel, active from 1854 to 1960. *Wroclaw, Poland.*
Facing: The abandoned, vandalized Storch synagogue. The inscription reads: The last hour of the Rabbi. *Wroclaw, Poland.*

Facing: A parchment from the Torah (Genesis 8:15) which had been cut by a Nazi to wear in his shoe. *Pomaz, Hungary.*
Below: Anti-Jewish inscription in German in the hallway of a building housing a Jewish club. *Krakow, Poland*

Facing: Street billboard announcing the performance of a play, "The Doctor Recommends Laughter," based on five short stories of Sholem Aleichem. *Odessa, U.S.S.R.* *Below*: Singers help celebrate the fifth night of Hanukkah. *Prague, Czechoslovakia.*

Facing: Actor prepares to perform *A Goldfadn Khulem* in Yiddish at the Jewish State Theater. *Warsaw, Poland.* *Below*: The *Purimspiel* is performed at the Yiddish State Theater. *Bucharest, Romania.*

Listening to Rov Wasserman read the Megillah Esther in
the kosher cantina. *Dorohoi, Romania*

Above: Students of Hebrew, both Jews and Catholics, listen to their Catholic instructor in the Jewish club. *Krakow, Poland*.
Facing: Zvi Segula teaching Yiddish in his home. *Krakow, Poland*.

Commemorating the one-month yartzeit of a friend. *Sofia, Bulgaria*.

Facing: Reading the "Amidah" prayer in the Beit Midrash
Dov Moshe "Zissu," named after the eminent Hasidic
rabbi. *Bucharest, Romania.*
Above: Man with his beard uncut in mourning for his
sister, who died two weeks before. *Bratislava, Czechoslovakia.*

Assistant Cantor Maxim Cohen chants the Haftorah. *Sofia, Bulgaria*.

Rabbi Daniel Meyer, the first rabbi in Czechoslovakia since 1964, leads the children in the lighting of the Hanukkah menorah. *Prague, Czechoslovakia.*

Rov Wasserman breaks a plate to signify the witnessing and signing of the ketubah. *Roman, Romania.*
Following pages:
Gypsy musicians, led by an Albanian violinist, play for the bride before her wedding. *Roman, Romania.*

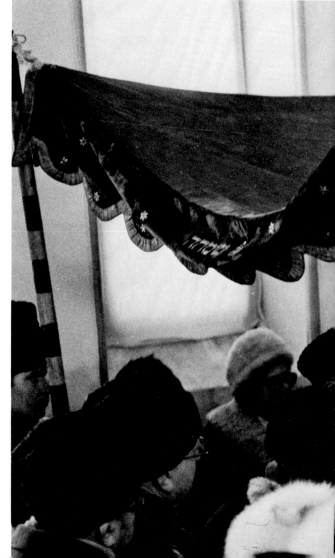

Facing: Rov Wasserman concludes his rather solemn droshe (sermon). *Roman, Romania.*
Below: Under the khupah, surrounded by a swarm of friends, the couple are wed, despite the cold of the synagogue. *Roman, Romania.*

Below: Young girl in the courtyard of the Beit Midrash. *Plovdiv, Bulgaria*.
Facing: Outside the Yiddish State Theater, in the old Jewish quarter. *Bucharest, Romania*

Facing: Chana Hap lighting Shabbat candles. *Budapest, Hungary.*
Below: Ina Liederman, daughter of Elizabeth and Gregori. This dissident family has been waiting most of Ina's life for emigration visas. *Kishinev, U.S.S.R.*

Facing, top: Children learning Hebrew in the heder of the Orthodox kehilla. *Budapest, Hungary.*

Above: Reading to children in the Jewish community center. *Belgrade, Yugoslavia.*

Left: In the Jewish communal hall, children celebrate Hanukkah. *Prague, Czechoslovakia.*

Above: A father and his child during the celebration of Tu B'Shevat. Behind them are portraits of young Jews who fought with Tito and the partisans during World War II. *Sarajevo, Yugoslavia.*

Facing: The Jewish Choir in the auditorium of the Popa Soare kosher cantina. *Bucharest, Romania.*

Below: The organizer and director of the National Conference on Jewry listening to Ladino and Yiddish folk music. *Belgrade, Yugoslavia.*

Bottom: Learning Hebrew in the Beit Midrash next to the Ohel Moshe synagogue. *Cluj, Romania.*

Facing top: Sunday morning Hebrew classes with students and teacher Itzkhak (Cara) Schwartz bundled against the cold. *Iasi, Romania.*

Facing, bottom: Itzkhak Gott, noted accordionist, bassist, and choral leader, rehearsing Iasi Symphonic Orchestra members for a performance of Yiddish and Hebrew folk music. *Iasi, Romania.*

Left: University students at the kosher cantina. *Cluj, Romania.*
Above: Oneg Shabbat. *Budapest, Hungary.*

Four children stand in synagogue courtyard. *Kishinev, U.S.S.R.*